# A Field Guide For Observing The Leadership of Change

*By* ***J.A. Schmid***

Copyright © 2008 by J.A. Schmid
All rights reserved

No part of this book may be reproduced in any form or by any electronic or mechanical means including information storage and retrieval systems, without permission in writing from the author. The only exception is by a reviewer, who may quote short excerpts in a review.

This book is a work of fiction. Names, characters, places, and incidents either are products of the author's imagination or are used fictitiously. Any resemblance to actual persons, living or dead, events, or locales is entirely coincidental.

J.A. Schmid
www.oakleafconsulting.com

Published in the United States of America
First Published: 2008
Second Edition Paperback – October 2014
EBook Edition – 2014

**Dedication**

To Jackie

# TABLE of CONTENTS

| | |
|---|---|
| INTRODUCTION | 1 |
| CHAPTER I – The Bells / The Voice / The Stories | 5 |
|     "Culture-Smulture!" | 6 |
|     Perceived Value | 7 |
|     The Genesis of Culture | 10 |
|     Show Time | 12 |
|     "Pay me now . . ." | 14 |
|     ". . . Or Pay Me Later." | 15 |
|     The Eye Exam | 16 |
|     The Shift | 19 |
|     "That ain't a bungee cord!" | 20 |
|     Ready / Set | 22 |
| CHAPTER II – THE SCOREBOARD | 25 |
|     "I'll tell you what . . ." | 26 |
|     "I thought I had a dream." | 29 |
|     "And the problem is . . ." | 30 |
|     "Sometimes the solution is staring you in the face." | 32 |
|     "A dead PIG?!?" | 33 |
|     Power up the "PIG" | 34 |
|     Share the Load | 35 |
|     Let them go. | 36 |
|     Mom wouldn't be pleased. | 37 |
|     The journey begins. | 39 |
|     "What we have here is a failure to communicate!" | 40 |
|     Values/Offerings/Segments | 41 |
| CHAPTER III – AFTER the VISION | 43 |
|     Is this a strategy, tactic, plan, mission, or what? | 45 |
|     "The Tormenting Triad & the Feisty Five" | 47 |
|     The 500-pound Turkey | 49 |
|     Does anyone know how to turn this thing on? | 51 |
|     Doing the right things right in the right order. | 53 |
|     An organization is its people. | 54 |
|     Concrete Feet | 55 |
|     "Whither?" | 56 |
|     "Yeah but!" | 57 |
|     The Rifling in the Barrel | 58 |
| CHAPTER IV – The LEADERSHIP PROCESS | 61 |
|     "I just don't get it." | 62 |
|     The PROCESS | 64 |

| | |
|---|---|
| The Sure Thing | 65 |
| The Bottle Rocket | 66 |
| The Journey Continues | 67 |
| "The Truth is Out There!" | 69 |
| "Out of the Closet" | 72 |
| Elephants, Tigers, and Bears . . . OH MY! | 73 |
| "If you don't do it, someone else will!" | 75 |
| **CHAPTER V – To CHARTER** | **79** |
| Churn Time | 81 |
| Chunk & Charter | 82 |
| 5W2H + 5Q's | 83 |
| "They what?!?! | 84 |
| You Make Your Own Luck! | 85 |
| The Paradox of Power | 87 |
| The Learning Zone | 88 |
| The Dark Side | 89 |
| Feeling the FORCE | 91 |
| **CHAPTER VI – To CHART** | **93** |
| "We want to be just like whom?" | 94 |
| "Queue Time" | 95 |
| The HIDDEN Organization | 97 |
| Success Feeds Success | 99 |
| "Off with their heads!" | 100 |
| The Truth only hurts when it's True | 102 |
| "Let's Get Together" | 102 |
| Feeling the Force | 104 |
| **CHAPTER VII – To CHALLENGE** | **105** |
| "You are not being purposeful!" | 107 |
| Defining the Problem | 108 |
| "Mirror, Mirror, on the wall . . . | 110 |
| " I wan'na be just like Mike!" | 112 |
| Stealing with Pride | 112 |
| "WHAT IF . . .?" | 114 |
| "WHY, WHY . . . WHY?" | 116 |
| Feeling the Force | 118 |
| **CHAPTER VIII – To CHANNEL** | **119** |
| Sharpen the blade! | 120 |
| Focus, Focus, Focus . . . | 122 |
| "Just the facts ma'am, just the facts." | 123 |
| What Now? | 125 |
| Concrete feet ain't all bad! | 126 |
| Channeling is Focus. | 127 |

| | |
|---|---|
| "That was quick!" | 129 |
| "This doesn't feel right." | 130 |
| Feeling the FORCE | 131 |
| **CHAPTER IX – To CHAMPION** | **133** |
| How did I get into this mess, Ollie? | 137 |
| You've got to undo what you did | 139 |
| We're going too FAST! | 141 |
| The sayer of sooths says this is an omen. | 142 |
| The answer is sometimes right under your nose. | 144 |
| Feeling the FORCE | 147 |
| **CHAPTER X – To CHECK** | **149** |
| You become what you measure! | 150 |
| THREE is a Lonely Number | 151 |
| The Paper Caper | 152 |
| Measure every which way. | 154 |
| Indicators are easy to see if you look. | 156 |
| Half baked is half baked | 158 |
| The Journey toward Wisdom | 159 |
| Déjà vu | 160 |
| The tools of the trade | 162 |
| An Invention isn't an Innovation | 163 |
| Feeling the FORCE | 165 |
| **CHAPTER XI – The HUMAN SIDE of IMPROVEMENT** | **167** |
| Show me the money! | 168 |
| That's all well & good . . . but this is about me! | 169 |
| Is there a leader in the house? | 172 |
| Getting to critical mass | 173 |
| Fear of Flying | 174 |
| Yeah . . . right! | 175 |
| Mastery | 176 |
| What you are isn't what you were or will be | 177 |
| **FINALE** | **179** |

## KNOWLEDGE IS POWER – PODER ES SERVIR

# INTRODUCTION

> *"How much wood*
> *Could a woodchuck chuck,*
> *If a woodchuck*
> *Could chuck wood?"*

I don't know the answer to this tongue twister. What I do know is that if a woodchuck could shift its perspective, and see the work of chucking wood as a process, then the woodchuck would have the potential to chuck a *lot* more wood than it originally could . . . if a woodchuck could chuck wood.

The same is true for us, *if* we can change our perspective (". . . get out of the box" or whatever you want to call it) and see our *work*, all that we do, as a *process*, particularly when we think about the act of leading or leadership.

*Leadership is a process*. It has inputs, a transform, and outputs that produce results. Management style (which is nothing more than management *behavior*) is a critical input to the leadership process. No matter how well-designed the process is, bad inputs will never produce great results. But the behavior of leadership, outside of cartoon strips, is seldom, if ever, dealt with upfront, during, or even after as a controlling aspect of the quality of outputs and resulting quality of results.

When is the last time you saw an organizational vision statement that didn't unequivocally state an aspiration to be #1? The core issue is always how this can be achieved. It takes a lot of things. It takes market knowledge, customer intimacy, technology, financial backing, and loyal, educated people...literally a critical mass of intelligence. Without fail, lack of success in advancing toward the #1 position is usually blamed on perceived deficiencies in one or more of the aforementioned areas. Accountability is thrust on the person(s) at the top, the leadership. Bad outcomes most often seem to translate to bad leadership. In my years of exposure to leadership, it is a rare case where you'll find a truly bad person in the role of a leader. Most often, you'll find good people in leadership roles that are trapped in a bad leadership process and, as a result, are practicing *survival* behaviors versus *leadership* behavior.

Central to all businesses, and transcending all boundaries, is the *leadership process* of organizations. The leadership process is the orderly way in which an organization's leaders engage their organization and orchestrate their organization's *outcomes*. The process of getting a decision or idea down to the action level where people can get their collective minds around it, clarify it and take action on it. A process approach has mainly been used in manufacturing focused on the operational aspects of an organization. Seldom is it ever deployed or thought about in the context of *leadership processes*.

Success or failure of leadership can be better understood through comparison to the Fire Triangle. To have a fire, three things must be present: oxygen, fuel, and heat. In a personal situation, leadership or otherwise, three things must be present for success: knowledge (I understand what is expected, I KNOW), resources (skill, time, ability, etc. – I am able to do what is expected, I CAN), and personal motivation (I want to do what is expected, I WILL). Just as in the fire triangle, if all three are not present, successful leadership cannot occur. This book deals with all three.

"I KNOW" is about understanding what leadership means in the context of an organization, and leadership's distinctive and additive role in an organization's success or lack of it. Many people are initially thrust into leadership roles because of their personal success in non-leadership roles, without ever having a definitive clue as to what leadership is about. They never understand what the new expectations of them are.

"I CAN" is not only about tools and theory, but also about *process*. Successful leadership involves a very disciplined and systematic process, not a barrage of "slap shots on goal," which is a tactic evident in many commonly practiced leadership techniques.

"I WILL" is about the disciplines of self-observance and self-audit: the ability to step back and see what you are doing and what impact it is having. It is rare to find a leader who, if they know what is expected and have the skills and the resources to do it, says "I WON'T." More common is leadership that either didn't know or couldn't, or didn't take the time to audit what it was they were doing and how it would impact the organization.

This book aims to heighten the awareness, the thinking, and the need for organizations and leadership to audit, elevate, and innovate their leadership behaviors and leadership work processes. Second-rate leadership behavior and leadership processes will not produce top results, regardless of the quality of the other inputs or process pieces, and vice versa.

This book is designed as a mental "clothes tree" to help organize the array of tools and techniques that most leaders have already been bombarded with, ones that, more often than not, clutter a leader's thinking. The pegs on the clothes tree are leadership behaviors. You'll find that any management technique or tool can be hung on at least one of the behavior pegs described in Chapters V through X, the *VERBS of CHANGE*.

As this book's title implies, leadership is something done in the field. So, when you pick a tool off the clothes tree, remember to demonstrate the behavior of the peg you took it from when using it in the field, out with your organization, rallying and leading it to its future success.

# CHAPTER I

## The Bells / The Voice / The Stories

Organizational *culture,* much has been said about this onerous subject. Every organization's got one. But, without doubt, it is an elusive creature to quantify, much less change. It's either the hero or the villain, but seldom anything in between. Organizations that have come face-to-face with increasingly competitive environments find themselves confronting a "culture change" sooner or later. But, before an organization's *culture* can be changed, what it exactly is, and how it came to be has to be understood.

An organization's *culture*, simply put, is the **norm of behavior** that describes the organizational responses toward its *primary stakeholders* (its Customers, its People, its Ownership, and the Society it comes in contact with). If you think about organizational behavior as normally distributed over a bell-shaped curve, it becomes easier to visualize and understand.

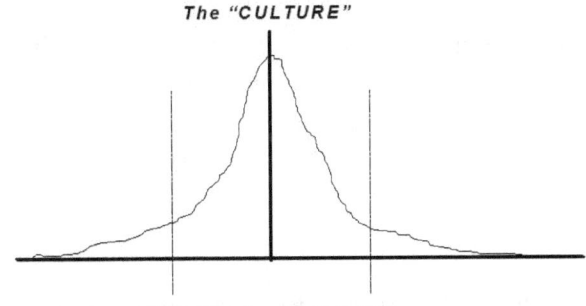

Organizations aren't made up of robots, and even if they were, there would always be some degree of variability. In any organization, different people respond differently to any given stimuli or situation. Yet, there is usually a degree of uniformity. If you measured and plotted, for example, how Company Z responds to a customer complaint, the responses would generally lie centered on some norm or typical behavior, which would be descriptive of Company Z's values about their customers and customer complaints. Just as in a normal distribution, where the bulk of the data lie within a relatively narrow band, there are always the "maverick" or outlying responses. These are the sources, or at least the opportunities, of organizational learning (organizational response, action, and outcomes, versus "typical" organizational response, action, and outcomes).

## *"Culture-Smulture!"*

Take the case of three different companies, all competing for the same order from the esteemed customer: Willie's Wiggly Lawn Ornaments Inc.

Willie's Wiggly Lawn Ornaments Inc. knows all three. Over the past several years, they have placed orders with all of them, leveraging one against the others for favorable pricing. But, Willie's Wiggly Lawn Ornaments Inc, during the past year, has been transforming itself. For example, it is now involving the people in its organization in the "Vendor Selection Process," and has granted a process ownership team the authority and accountability for this year's *glopata* contracts.

The three vendor companies have come in fairly close on pricing. So, as far as Wiggly Lawn Ornaments Inc.'s senior purchasing guru Sam (who had singularly handled all the *glopata* procurement in the past) is concerned, "Why not, this is simple math," and Sam wanted to be thought of as an empowering kind of person anyway.

Sam had decided not to waste time with the Vendor Selection Process Team: ". . . meetings are so useless." But, Sam did decide to sit in during the closure meeting for the annual *glopata* contract as a process observer. After all, Sam was still the one who would have to write and execute the contracts, and Sam was, in fact, a part of the process (albeit up until now the-tail-that-wags-the-dog).

During the closure meeting, it became clear that engineering, operations, and accounting overwhelmingly endorsed one company's products and services. Before Sam could wise up to what was about to happen, the empowered team had thrown 100% *glopata* share to Arlans General Co., leaving Haggle Corp. and Higgles Power Zone Inc. out in the cold.

To top it all off, Arlans General Co. came in with the highest unit price, and Higgles Power Zone Inc. had arranged their annual weekend fishing outing with Sam for the coming weekend.

As the meeting broke up and people filed out of the room (all genuinely concerned whether Sam was feeling O.K.), Sam simply sat there and wondered what the hell had just happened. Even Sam's last-ditch admonishments for the need for proper documentation didn't slow the runaway team. Everything Sam asked for would be there ". . . in the morning." Sam's apple cart had just been made road-kill by **corporate culture**. What the documentation in the morning would ultimately show was that the Arlans General Co. *corporate customer culture* offered *value* much greater than the *price* they were selling *glopata* at, particularly in the context of the value/price relationships offered by Haggle Corp. and Higgles Power Zone Inc.

## *Perceived Value*

Pictured graphically here are the three distinct *corporate customer cultures* that Wiggly Lawn Ornaments Inc.'s Vendor Selection Process had uncovered during their evaluation.

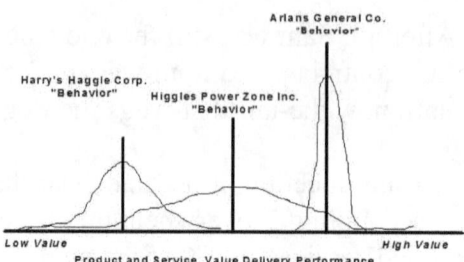

Haggle Corp., while consistent, was still behaving the way they had for the last twenty years ("Why fix what isn't broke!"). They were still arrogant about competition ("We were here a long time before they came on the scene, and we'll be here long after they're gone!"). And, they never respected Wiggly Lawn Ornaments Inc.'s evolving needs as Wiggly's customers' expectations changed ("Pink Flamingos just aren't enough!").

Higgles Power Zone Inc., on the other hand, seemed to be having an identity crisis. They were implementing just about every customer-friendly initiative that came down the pike, but their response was so diverse and variable it was unbearable. If you got the right person at Higgles Power Zone Inc., it was great, but you were just as likely to get someone who must have just jumped ship from Haggle Corp.

In the case of Arlans General, they were an organization that had been operating for years, and one that also had chronic problems. But, they had, in the last two years, really gotten their act together. Their tech reps and R&D engineers were now always collaborative and open when approached by Wiggly Lawn Ornaments Inc.'s new product design group. When they had met to discuss development changes, Arlans' General's people handled every verbal agreement at these meetings as a contract. When Wiggly Lawn Ornaments Inc. placed an order, regardless of size, Arlans' General delivered what they promised: product, service, and timing. And, if there ever was a problem, someone was on the scene pronto. In addition, their product (while unit costs were higher) gave Wiggly Lawn Ornaments Inc. better yields and productivity, so their total cost of using Arlans' *glopata* was better, even at their higher unit prices. Arlans was even the one that had suggested the Vendor

Quality auditing process to Wiggly Lawn Ornaments Inc., and had helped the Wiggly Lawn Ornaments Inc. Vendor Selection Process team learn to use it.

Arlans' General was acting like an ally, not the adversary that Haggle Corp. was consistently, and that Higgles Power Zone was on more than random occasions.

Suddenly, Sam was faced with the unenviable position of trying to explain to the two disenfranchised companies why it was exactly that they wouldn't be getting *any* *glopata* business from Wiggly Lawn Ornaments Inc. during the coming year. In the past, Sam's life had been easy -- *price*. Sam was, by consensus, a world-class "price-hammer," skilled at playing multiple suppliers.

Sam wondered to himself whether the team's decision ought to be brought up this weekend during the fishing trip with Haggle Corp. But reason prevailed, and Sam decided that bad news was best not delivered out in the middle of a wilderness lake, particularly when the boat wasn't yours. Sam concluded that after the weekend would be soon enough to get back together with the team and find out more about this "corporate culture thing."

What Sam would discover, in time, is that **corporate culture** is the culmination of people *emulating the behaviors of their leaders*. A leader in this case is the person an individual sees as the holder of their individual punishment or rewards. Most individuals mold their behaviors to stay within the "comfort zone" of their leader. Those people who can't or won't mold their behavior to that comfort zone ultimately move on down the road in search of another leader and an environment where they do "fit." The old Mother Goose rhyme says it all. "Birds of a feather flock together, so do pig and swine, but rats and mice will have their choice and so shall I have mine." The same is true for organizations and corporations. The people of an organization watching their leader's behavior and emulating it in their own individual behaviors are the wellspring of **corporate culture**.

## *The Genesis of Culture*

What is it that people watch and interpret that drives their collective behavior and ultimately defines **corporate culture**?

People pay attention to three things, and their alignment with each other. The three are the *bells*, the *voice,* and the *stories* of an organization.

The *bells* are what attract an organization's attention. They are those things that an organization's leaders write, speak, and talk about, the things they declare as critically important.

The *voice* that leads an organization is the actions and behaviors of its leaders (whether aligned or misaligned) as they relate to what they said was important.

And finally, the *stories* that guide an organization are its verbal histories, its oral traditions of those instances where choices were made (aligned or not) around the bells that have been rung. The force behind all three is **values**.

In today's competitive environment, there isn't a company around that hasn't rung the bell loudly about customer satisfaction in their vision or mission statements. After all, who is going to do business with someone who won't declare customer satisfaction one of their top priorities?

This *bell* is usually amplified by a series of coffee mugs, banners, hats, T-shirts and accessories, rallies, etc. It's in the annual reports; it's everywhere (for awhile anyway) shortly after the bell's been rung.

But, after the bell stops resonating, people begin to listen for the **voice**. People aren't fools. They've been burned before. They watch for their leader's responses to the bell. Sure, their leader ensured they all watched the videos, collected the mugs, went to the rally, and wore their T-shirts on "show day." But the voice that leads with respect to customer satisfaction is not about that. The voice that leads is the action and behavior of the leader the next time a customer visits, or the next time there is a decision to make about releasing some questionable product, or the next time a customer calls with a complaint.

The value that has been declared through the ringing of the bell is clear. What's equally clear is that no one can own a value until they've paid for it.

Paying for it in this context is done through the expenditure of each leader's time and energy, what they say yes to and, often more importantly, what they say *no* to in their daily actions.

Owning a value (in this case customer satisfaction) isn't a one-time, lump-sum payment kind of thing. Value ownership is a continuum of payments, sometimes big, sometimes small, but, regardless of size or the length of time payments have been made, if a leader misses one, they no longer own that value. The bell that was rung is silenced with a much stronger sound: the **voice that leads** when a leader misses a payment. The *missed payment* becomes a **story** that will invariably trickle down and impact any number of future decisions.

However, as a rule of thumb, organizations generally give their leaders *up to 48 hours* to make up for a *missed payment.* Beyond this time limit, integrity is questioned and the damage is generally done. Although *late* payments always have a heavy "interest payment" attached to them (a personal admission that "I really messed up. I just wasn't thinking when I did that. Thanks for calling me on it!"), late payments are a way of salvaging some good out of a situation gone bad. While there may be an organizational expectancy of perfection from their leadership, there is also an organizational pragmatism that does allow for mistakes, but . . .

## Show Time

Let's take the case of Joe "BA" Hurang; the CEO at Higgles Power Zone Inc. Joe had recently been to a "charm" school.

Joe listened to all the testimonials about how to improve performance by taking a new direction with customers. It was no longer an arms-length, "take what we make and be happy" kind of business environment. Getting close to customers was a survival issue. He came back to Higgles Power Zone Inc. with a passion to act. He declared himself a true believer and wanted to "do something" quickly.

Jim Spin, Higgles Power Zone Inc.'s HR VP, jumped in with both feet. He had heard, through his network, all about the "big show events" going on in other companies, and this was the chance he was waiting for.

Within weeks, Higgles Power Zone Inc. had a big "Revival Rally" featuring Joe and his new "True Beliefs," with Jim Spin acting as the interlocutor. It was videotaped, and copies, including scripts, were sent to all the remote locations so that everyone in the company could stage their own site Revival Rallies and "get the message."

Purchasing had found some great deals for prepackaged "Customer Focus" gear, complete with slogans, graphics, and posters; and, for a minimal charge, they could even get the Higgles Power Zone Inc. company logo silk-screened onto the T-shirts. Everything went great and, with lots of back slapping, Joe's staff declared victory. They all agreed that this was indeed one of Higgles Power Zone Inc.'s greatest moments.

At the following Friday morning staff meeting, Jim Spin reviewed all the reaffirming feedback, carefully screening out any cynicism. Everyone in that staff meeting would privately reflect later that "old Joe" sure looked like the boy who just stuck in his thumb and pulled out the proverbial plum at the staff meeting that day. Joe felt liberated. He'd done the right thing. With that, Joe "BA" Hurang rewarded himself with a long weekend. It had been a physically draining event, and he'd earned a rest.

There were a lot of stories told about Joe, enough parts of them true that almost everyone accepted them as 100% gospel fact. "BA" stood for "Bad-Ass." Joe had earned it over the years coming up through the ranks by taking "tough" stands, particularly with customers, suppliers, and employees in the name of the "bottom line."

The time "old Joe" turned a plant screw up (where he was manager) into a coup was a legend. Two things Joe could do well were 1.) Think on his feet; and 2.) Speak. One morning, right in the middle of Joe's plant staff meeting, a customer called, complaining about the shipment they'd just received. Factually, the shipment was "marginal," but Joe had ordered it shipped anyway. "Too close to the end of the month. It will mess up our P&L performance." Within ten minutes on the speaker phone, with all Joe's staff as witnesses, Joe had the customer convinced it was they who were inept and at fault, and apologizing for interrupting Joe's busy day. Joe was one smart, tough cookie.

There were other stories, equally convincing (you just don't get the "BA" label for a single event) that allowed people to feel comfortable that they knew what "old Joe" really wanted. What many people sense but may never be able to articulate is that the stories organizations keep alive about themselves and their leaders are, in fact, the inertial guidance system of that organization's culture. Stories are what keep organizations "on track." Stories are what people fall back on (consciously or unconsciously) for direction in the myriad of decisions they make when confronted with solving daily problems.

*"Pay me now..."*

Back to Joe "BA" Hurang, CEO at Higgles Power Zone Inc. Joe came back to work early Monday (after his long weekend) feeling energized and on top of his game. The first thing he noticed was that someone had written a 9:00 am customer visit on his calendar.

Now, everybody knew that Joe blocked his calendar off on purpose until 10 am on Mondays so he could get caught up on what had been going on over the weekend at the plants. Joe bellowed out to his secretary El (who had just filled a new "Customers are #1" mug with freshly-brewed coffee) that whoever overwrote his calendar must be some new kid on the block, and Joe further stated that from now on only El and he had the authority to change his calendar. And there was one last request before he disappeared into his inner sanctuary for the next three hours. "Call whoever it was that did this and tell them that A) I'm NOT coming, and B) . . . consider it their lucky day because I'm not going to hunt them down and tear them a new one for screwing with my calendar."

Joe had just missed his first payment (and he thought his account was already paid in full). Joe's bell ringing had really opened some new doors, and after he left early Friday for his long weekend, a sales manager and a counterpart in R&D had really jumped at the opportunity.

There was a particularly tough account with which Higgles Power Zone Inc. had done next to no business at all for several years. Every sales call was always greeted with the question: "Is old BA still in charge?" They had hesitantly agreed to come in on Monday, but only after hearing in detail about how Joe had changed, and about the new era he had introduced at the rally. They were in the planning stages of a new product line, and were willing to discuss the possibilities of Higgles Power Zone Inc. participating in the development phase. Part of the interaction Sales and R&D had promised was to have the "new Joe" greet the customer and give them a condensed presentation of the substance of the rally first thing Monday morning.

El called down with the "news," but there was no turning back. No matter what they said, El wasn't about to let them go in to see "old Joe" and explain; furthermore, El felt deceived by "you two clowns," and that was the last time El was ever going to change Joe's calendar because of one of their "harebrained" requests. End of discussion!

El had gotten to this position by being a good "gatekeeper," and she knew that Joe's philosophy was that two points make a straight line. There was no way in the world El was going to risk putting another point on the board for Joe to connect.

What had just occurred, although Joe never realized it, was an alignment check. Joe's bell was clear -- Customer Satisfaction was Higgles Power Zone Inc.'s top priority. The stories about Joe were equally clear, although 180° away from the bell (". . . don't leave anything on the table that can go to this month's bottom line"). What people were now waiting and listening for was the voice that leads, and they heard that loud and clear. Joe's action, his voice, wasn't aligned with Joe's bell. Joe's action ("I'm NOT coming") was still in alignment with the stories of "old Joe."

"*. . . Or Pay Me Later.*"

So, months later, when the responses were tallied from a blind customer survey (a new MBA recruit had commissioned it, impressed by Joe's passion at the Rally), why was Joe surprised and shocked when Higgles Power Zone Inc. got rated slightly above bird cage paper?

The root cause lies in Joe's personal leadership misalignment. Several cartoon strips make a practice of poking fun at leadership misalignment. These cartoons wouldn't be funny if it weren't for the fact that leadership misalignment is so prevalent (from business to government to interest to political groups). The fact that many organizational leaders don't ever audit whether their *bells*, *voice*, and *stories* are all tracking over the same ground is a leadership trait that advances the popularity of these kinds of cartoon strips. The fact that *bells* ringing one way and voices sounding the other way are so commonplace it ensures these cartoon strips will have a long life.

In change situations, where organizational leaders are trying to create a new culture, a new norm of behavior, to make their organization more competitive, success or failure hinges on whether the leaders themselves are the first to get their **voice**, and the first to create new **stories** (the new oral tradition), and on whether both voice and stories are aligned with the **bells** that they ring.

What could old "BA" Joe have done differently? First, he could have recognized the dynamic of his own words, actions, and deeds, and their inseparable interplay with his company's culture.

If Joe had been wiser, he would have jumped at the opportunity Higgles Power Zone Inc.'s Sales and R&D mangers had presented to him in order to create (through his actions, his **voice**) a new story to be told about the bell he'd just rung. It would have been told for years to come how Joe had dropped his sacred Monday morning retreat in an instant to spend time with a customer. Second, Joe could have (if he had known) evoked the *48*-Hour rule to make up for the *missed payment*. Although the *late* payment in this case would also include an external customer, and the "interest payment" attached to it would be huge in terms of Joe's personal time (maybe hopping a plane and arriving at the customer's shop, hat in hand, with an apology) it would be an effective way of salvaging some good out of a bad situation. The late payment would make for a strong voice and an aligned story. But most importantly, what "old Joe" had said versus what he'd done had really tarnished his integrity. The organization was positively going to be slow on the uptake the *next* time "old Joe" tried introducing a change.

## *The Eye Exam*

In Joe's defense, he was as intelligent and dedicated as they come. He really had meant everything he had said at his corporate

"Revival Rally." The problem was that he didn't understand what he had said *really meant*. To the organization, it meant that "old Joe" had just changed their "vision prescription," and had ordered a new set of "lenses" to view and observe themselves through.

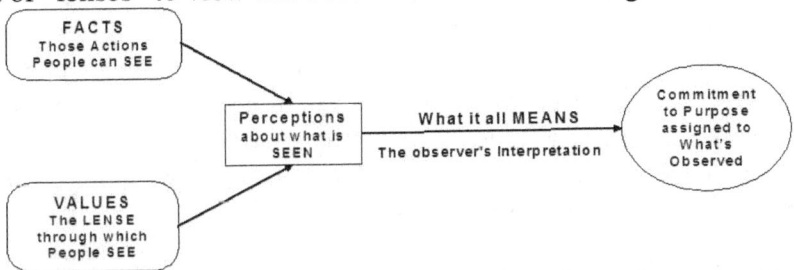

The simple model presented here describes what would have been going on in the Revival Rally participants' minds. First, "old Joe" had disavowed all the old sacred customer norms and **Values** that had gotten Higgles Power Zone Inc. to this point in its history, saying they just weren't good enough to see them through the next period of their history.

Customer intimacy, customer driven quality, customer satisfaction are the new rules of the game. "NO more arms length. Let's get up close and personal!" When the people of Higgles Power Zone Inc. used these *new values* or lenses, they could see that pretty much everything they had been doing around customers was going to have to change.

The **Facts** were clear. People leaving the Rally were overheard saying things like, "I guess this means accounting's not going to be the lead in handling customer complaints anymore," and, "Does this mean we'll get to meet customers?" People were beginning to articulate a new set of *facts* that, when perceived through these new lenses, would cause Higgles Power Zone Inc. to take on the **Presence** of a "customer friendly" company. And when that Presence was combined with the **Commitment** to Higgles Power Zone Inc.'s **Purpose**, their roles and their behavior took on a whole new *meaning* and *interpretation.*

Come Monday morning, "old Joe's" refusal to give up his Monday morning ritualistic retreat in order to meet with a customer was a *FACT*. When viewed through the old lenses of Higgles Power Zone Inc.'s old *values*, it wasn't even an event ("same-old-same-old"). Joe's *action* was who the "old" Higgles was. But, when viewed through the new *Value* lenses that Joe had introduced, Joe's Monday morning refusal was outrageous. In the aftermath of Monday morning, the Higgles people who had seen it happen or heard about it had to go through a reconciliation of what they had just witnessed. Either Higgles was going to be what it always had been and people knew it to be, or Higgles was going to be the company "old Joe" said it needed to become.

People had genuinely been destabilized by the Revival Rally, and they needed to re-stabilize around something. Those who wanted to move forward cited Joe's VOICE in staging and carrying the "Revival Rally" on his back, discounting the Monday morning event as a simple misunderstanding. Those who were more comfortable keeping things the way they had been, and knew how to be successful in that environment, quickly pointed to Joe's VOICE in staying in his office and ignoring the customer visit.

What transpired out of all this in the months that followed, seen through the eyes of Higgles Power Zone Inc.'s customers, was response and behavior out of Higgles that ranged all over the map. Customers were concerned and confused. Who was Higgles now? They had learned how to deal with the "old Joe" culture, but this was something different entirely.

While customers didn't particularly like the "old Joe" culture, it was known, and being known it was trusted (at least to the point where they knew what to expect). Customers wanted to believe and trust in the new Higgles Power Zone Inc., but stories were rampant about people getting slammed when the deeper, darker, "old Joe" culture emerged out of the shadows. So, what they all did, to varying degrees, was begin to tone down their orders and take a wait and see approach with Higgles. The Higgles culture curve had just flattened out, and the Higgles norm of behavior toward customers that had once been pretty clear and relatively narrowly defined was now spread over a wide spectrum. Some days they acted like the best of Arlans' General; other days you were just as likely to get a response equivalent to the worst of Haggle Corp.

The preceding example, although highly over-simplified and probably more dramatized than a soap opera, does serve in illustrating how organizational culture comes to be, and, more importantly, the dynamics of how and why it evolves or changes (or doesn't change). There ought to be a realization or awareness that every leadership action that is observed is interpreted in the context of organizational values, and that each action either supports the change that has been initiated or undermines it.

## *The Shift*

Culture change describes shifting an organization from one behavioral "comfort zone" to another. The reality is that it is no more work to be in one culture than it is to be in any other. Work, just as in physics, is expended by moving from one comfort zone to the next. In many cases, this is evolutionary, and isn't sensed until much later when individuals look back over an extended history. Evolutionary change is fine, but <u>*only*</u> if the competitive environment allows a relatively long period of time for an organization's culture to respond and change. Yet, *speed* is a competitive weapon that is more talked about than truly cultivated as an attribute, particularly in the context of evolving an organization's culture.

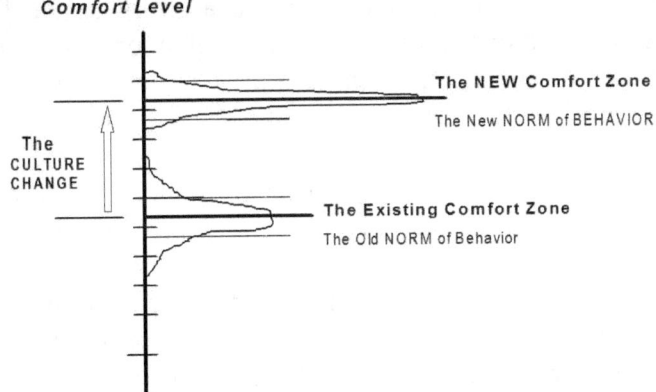

Many leading companies are very willing to open up their corporate cultures to anyone who is interested in seeing them. It is almost an in-your-face competitive tactic. They can do that without fear because the facts are clear. A "new and improved" Organizational Culture is one of, if not the most, difficult attributes for any organization to attain, particularly "higher competitive forms" that are significant deviations from "typical experience." The farther the deviation from "typical," the harder it is for a would-be competitor to "catch."

Some organizations recruit away a "change leader" from the organization whose culture they are trying to emulate, with mixed results. The new "initiative" leader (most times entering in an ad hoc position), undoubtedly destabilizes their new organization with a different set of behaviors well outside the existing norm of behaviors. Many times the results are degrees of discomfort best described as "corporate acid indigestion."

However, the stories and the voices that lead organizations are not the ad hoc leaders, but are the ongoing behaviors of the incumbent line leadership. No doubt bringing in an ad hoc change agent was thought to be a way to present a strong **voice**, but in almost all instances the act of bringing in someone new is perceived *only* as a loud **bell** of the incumbent leadership.

## *"That ain't a bungee cord!"*

If the incumbent leadership fails to act further and fails to become the first to move to the new sets of behaviors introduced by the change agent, the organization isn't about to go anywhere, and the "import" crashes and burns in a relatively short period of time.

It is analogous to taking an organization to the brink of a deep crevice and ordering them to jump to the other side. If fear is an organizational driver, then many people might try to do just that: jump. For sure, the new change leader will try to go. But the "leash" of leadership behavior is relatively short, and before those who took a running leap toward the other side of the crevice can get there, the "leash" pulls them up short and drops them dangling in the crevice, hanging on for dear life.

This leadership style - "JUMP" - is only effective in crisis situations where the "danger" of not jumping is "clear and present." More effective, but not always, is to bring that same organization again to the brink of the crevice. The incumbent leader is the first to go, saying "FOLLOW ME!" Unfortunately, it is not as simple as that either. The problem is that the "leash" is still there, and it's just as likely to jerk the incumbent leaders back into the crevice and have them hanging on for dear life as it is for those who, in the former case, were ordered to jump. The "leash," in all cases, is the intertwined congruent **bells & voice & stories** that form the organization's existing **culture**, its existing accepted norm of behavior.

Take, for example, the simple cultural evolution of "office-dress-down-day" (it has pretty well infiltrated every corporate culture in the U.S., but was a huge shock when first introduced). There are great stories that are told around the corporate campfires about "opening day," stories of people who "tried," but got abruptly caught at the end of the "leadership leash" with "inappropriate" dress, and of the "mavericks" who continue to push the limits.

For those who can remember, how organizations "managed office-dress-down-day" is an excellent illustration of the "leash" and a grand opportunity to compare a number of different organizational "cultures" on the same field.

How empowering can an organization that assumes their people can't exercise enough good judgment to dress themselves appropriately for the function they will fill each day, and feels they must intervene with rules and codes possibly be??

Or, what kind of organization is it where people would deliberately dress in ways that do not support that organization's interests?

Are dress-down rules the last tangible remnant of the old vertical power culture, a forgotten piece of the old "leash," or are they a misaligned "voice"? What statement (*bell* or *voice*) is being made with or without strict rules? How much does an organization value diversity when dress rules are narrowly defined? Has an organization ever consciously dealt with the cultural aspect of office dress, and how that aspect supports or fails to support the organization's aspirations, and communicated it in a way that indicated it accepted ownership?

Or, was "dress-down" dealt with in an ad hoc manner because "everyone else" was doing it? Answers to these questions and a plethora of others can give an organization or an organization's watchers real insights and leads into exploring "culture."

### *Ready / Set*

The "leash" exists, and will always exist. It isn't necessarily a bad thing. It is only a problem in *change situations*.

So, HOW do organizations deal with their current "leash" and move on to new cultures and forms in an orderly way, while creating a new "leash" that will again provide the new order that is needed? Moving an organization's culture, getting to a new (and hopefully more competitive) norm of behavior is more about READY / SET than it is about GO. Getting ready is about leadership engaging their organization in objectively cataloging and measuring the organization's current culture, its current *bells, voice, and stories*. Only after this has been done should the leadership begin the process of defining the **culture** that strategically will be competitively superior in terms of its new *bells, voice, and stories*. In this context, the behavioral shifts can more easily be articulated and understood. This context also provides the stage for effective communication when the shifts are initiated, and for dealing with resistance that will always be present.

In culture change situations, organizational leaders often rush to confront organizational resistance without first examining their own personal resistance, and without understanding how their behavior, *the voice that leads*, impacts and ultimately controls the rate and amount of change that can be realized. A personal audit of **MY** **bells**, **voice**, and **stories** is something best done in the beginning rather than at the end. To avoid the costs of false starts and recycles, remember the old adage, "The wise do in the beginning what fools do in the end," and see your own mistakes before they happen.

# CHAPTER II

## "A Tricky Little Game"
## THE SCOREBOARD

The concept of a multidimensional corporate *scoreboard* has been introduced and reintroduced for decades to the business community. It states that future business success must be driven and measured through a scoreboard that tracks the value creation for a business's four primary constituents, a.k.a. stakeholders.

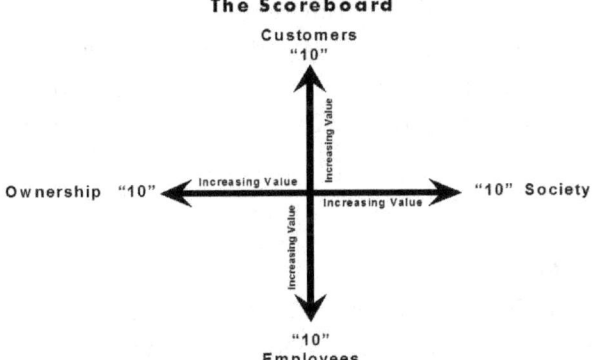

The operating principle that accompanies this concept is that "points" cannot be added to one dimension / constituent of the scoreboard by taking away points from another dimension / constituent. This scoreboard concept is perceived by many as a significant departure from the norm of business measurement that focuses one-dimensionally on financial performance for **ownership**.

The articulation of a multidimensional scoreboard is relatively new, but the notion isn't. In reality, it has always been there. What has changed, in part, are the expectations of all stakeholders. What was a "10" a decade ago may in fact be rapidly approaching a "0" today. Expectations driven by the "competitive" introduction of new possibilities brought the other "***silent three***" to the forefront, with the dimension of *ownership* simultaneously continuing to move toward even more demanding definitions of "value." Along with increased expectations, the scoring "rules" have changed.

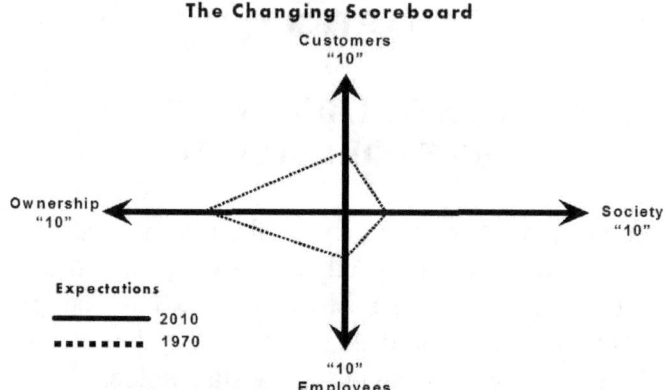

Pictured here are the scoring levels of several decades ago, overlaid with the expectation levels and "rules" of today's business environment. The area within the lines expanded due to increasing societal expectations, employee expectations, and customer expectations.

## *"I'll tell you what . . ."*

"Back in the day," it was pretty much enough for a business to "just be there" in order to fulfill its role as a viable part of **society**. Many of today's symbols of environmental *risk* (e.g. smokestacks, cooling towers, etc.) were once seen as a community's *totems* of success.

With occasional acts of philanthropy and goodwill, most businesses filled their "obligations" of citizenry, and managed "high scores" without a whole lot of thought or effort. Today, the dimensions of a business's covenant with the society in which it resides have dramatically changed.

A covenant can be thought of as an agreement or obligation between unequals that is fulfilled with some degree of sacrifice. In today's climate, the poles of inequality have, in some cases, been reversed. Today, just "being there" isn't enough. Where decades ago the "sacrifice" to fulfill the covenant was most often "offered up" by the community, in many cases the "sacrifice" is now increasingly being "offered up" by the business. The realities of business displacement, and the search for a society in which the poles are still as they once were are current measures of this dimension's dynamic.

"Back in the day," the notion of a captive work force was the norm. The **employee** "covenant" was relatively easy to maintain, and the surface of the "playing field" was flat, with well-defined "bounds" and markers that only the unenlightened or truly greedy tried to ignore.

The true mobility, and indeed the expectation within the workforce of mobility, has been accelerated by the "downsizing" and business migrations of the last decades. The employee dimension is rapidly undergoing a polarity shift in who offers the sacrifice to fulfill it. Forecasts continue to predict that the single largest restraint to a business's growth will be that business's ability to attract and retain people. Long gone are the days of just "putting up a sign" in the window or an ad in the local paper. Skilled workers and even effective entry-level workers are getting harder and harder to come by in many regions of the world. And it isn't only a supply and demand issue that is driving the hurtle rate of the employee dimension. It is increasing pressures from dual income families and single parents, to medical coverage, to even the rising expectation of a "fun place to work" (which not too long ago was oxymoronic) that are driving the new definitions of a perfect "10."

"Back in the day," **Customer** satisfaction was or wasn't an issue, depending on where you were in the value chain, and who had the "power." Captive regions and customer groups have been relegated to a memory with global competition. The definitions of "value" are changing in this dimension more rapidly than in any of the other dimensions. A "10" a decade ago was a good product at a good price. Product Life Cycles then were defined in terms of years (remember Experience Curves) and now, in some sectors, they are defined in terms of months. Value chains are in constant turmoil from dealing with this new definition of speed.

Whether leaders were exposed to the scoreboard concept or not they all feel its presence. Most tried to situationally deal with it and had some success, but very few internalized the implications, and fewer yet attempted to holistically integrate or critically review their own organizations.

Many did superficially, declared victory, and moved on, only to be bitten later. Some leaders saw merit in the concept, found deficiencies, and undertook initiatives to "fix" this or that piece. Others, though, have gone back and not only looked at their vision statements for inclusion of all four constituents, but have also gone through the more demanding task of reconciling each opposite the other three. Those leaders that did discovered that the *voice that leads*, their *actions*, had become an order of magnitude more complicated than ever before. The reason was that now every action would be viewed through four different and equally demanding sets of "value" lenses, and interpreted differently.

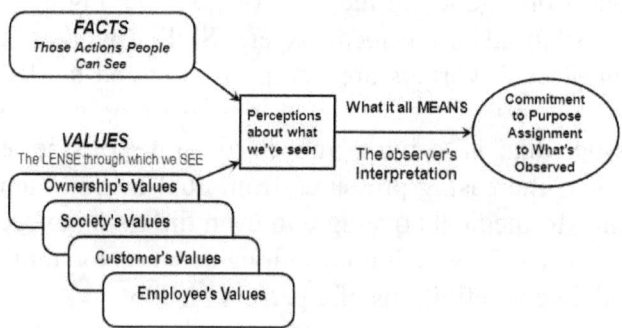

Those who tried to treat each set of values situationally would invariably end up being "called" by one or even all three of the other stakeholders. It became a game of "hot potato" in a number of cases.

***"I thought I had a dream."***

Let's take a look at Willie's Wiggly Lawn Ornaments. Willie (the founder, president and current CEO of Wiggly) had gotten into the business basically because of his childhood fascination and obsession with the pink flamingo lawn ornaments owned by a neighbor down the street. He'd never seen a pink flamingo in real life. He'd been amazed by the Sunday night Disney presentations that focused on the wilds of Africa, programs showing skies transformed by pink, vibrant masses of these birds. It wasn't until college that he realized there were actually pink flamingos resident in parts of the U.S. After college graduation, and being disappointed by the fact that the world hadn't automatically become his "oyster," Willie went to work by day as a bank teller. But by night, he was Willie the dreamer, working on developing the ultimate Pink Flamingo lawn ornament.

Without belaboring the point, Willie started the business and grew it, moving from local, to national, to international, redefining his business many times along the way in terms of its offerings and distribution channels. Wiggly Lawn Ornaments Inc. manufactured most of their products within a 100-mile radius of where he'd been born. They had expanded their product offerings on several occasions through resale from manufacturers in Asia. Some of these same suppliers had seen the light, and were now bypassing Wiggly Lawn Ornaments Inc. and going direct. One in particular had become a formidable competitor. Willie was feeling hard-pressed. Their main market access channel was through a "mega-store" retailer, who, while still preferential to Willie, was bringing a lot of pressure to bear about the breadth of Wiggly Lawn Ornaments Inc.'s product line and price.

Willie really was agitated. This would be a lot easier if he hadn't gone public a few years back to fund expansion. Willie was getting all tangled up in the "web" of the **scoreboard**. The easy financial way out was to move the factory equipment into lower cost labor markets. Wiggly Lawn Ornaments Inc. wasn't a permanent, investment-intensive business, and was (as Willie began to think about it) very portable. While relocation would take care of some customer pricing pressures, and sure looked great on the financial study spreadsheets, a move like that would be devastating to the people of Wiggly Lawn Ornaments Inc. Some he had grown up with and had signed on with him in the beginning. This had always been a "family business," and Wiggly Lawn Ornaments Inc. had just begun to hire third generation employees. What would become of them? What would the community response be? He and his wife weren't going to move. Would he still maintain his "pillar" status? Maybe he should just retire and claim "I'm not to blame" when the new management took the "obvious" moves. If Willie tried to hang on to the way Wiggly Lawn Ornaments Inc. had been, the end would probably come a lot sooner than he even wanted to think about, and that end would be just as disastrous for the employees and the community, and for his personal fortunes as well.

## "And the problem is . . ."

Willie began doodling on a piece of paper, and scratched out what appears here. He came to the realization that there was an interdependence and interplay between and among those constituents that had a stake in the outcome of Wiggly Lawn Ornaments Inc. He also recognized that any action he took would be viewed by each, but from a different set of values, and that if he was going to pull this off and feel good about himself, whatever he did needed to satisfy all four. The way Willie began to look at it was that the **COST** of saying YES to whatever it was he'd do was Wiggly's having to say NO to an endless list of other options.

Willie also concluded that this "business" of leadership was all about maximizing the ***inequalities*** for each of the stakeholders through the same action. In other words, the perceived Value for each of the four would have to be far greater than the interpreted Price they must pay, which in turn must be far greater than Wiggly Lawn Ornaments Inc.'s COST of doing it.

In the case of Customers, the Value of doing business with Wiggly Lawn Ornaments Inc. would have to be seen as far greater than the Price they must pay for what Wiggly offered (in the context of competitive alternatives), which in turn must be far greater than the Cost of Wiggly providing it.

Regarding Wiggly Lawn Ornaments Inc. employees, the perceived Value of being part of Wiggly would have to be far greater than the Price they paid for not pursuing other employment opportunities, versus the Cost of Wiggly providing them with employment.

```
                    VALUE
                     to
                  CUSTOMERS
                     ∨
                     ∨
                   "PRICE"
                     ∨
   VALUE             ∨                VALUE
    to    >> "PRICE" >> COST << "PRICE" <<   to
 OWNERSHIP           ∧               SOCIETY
                   "PRICE"
                     ∧
                    VALUE
                     To
                  EMPLOYEES
```

With respect to the Wiggly Lawn Ornaments Inc. stockholders, the Value of investing in Wiggly would have to be perceived as far greater than their Cost of not investing in other investment opportunities, and in turn would have to be far greater than Wiggly's expense of executing the "game plan."

And finally, the communities in which Wiggly Lawn Ornaments Inc.'s operations resided would have to see the Value of Wiggly's continued presence as far greater than the Price of their continued support that, in turn, was far greater than Wiggly's Cost of staying.

As Willie began to see it, this was really a "tricky little game." Willie began to wonder why he was the one stuck with all of this. Instead of allowing the other stakeholders to get away with a "passive" role in what was happening and having them judging and second-guessing his every move, maybe he ought to somehow engage them so that they shared ownership in the decisions, and the outcomes as well. But, if he did, wouldn't they all see it as a sign of weakness? Maybe a move like that would only accelerate the situation and move it from bad to worse more quickly. With that thought, Willie decided to run down to his favorite lunch spot, the Armadillo Grill, and grab a bite to eat.

### *"Sometimes the solution is staring you in the face."*

When Willie walked into the Armadillo Grill, a poster in the entryway caught his eye. It was the Armadillo Grill's Vision Statement. As he waited to be seated, he read through it, and in it the Armadillo clearly laid out its expectations of what it wanted to be and do for all four of its stakeholders. Willie didn't remember ever seeing it there before, so after he was seated he inquired with the waiter if Steph, the owner, was there, and told him that he'd sure appreciate a minute. Willie knew Steph well. She and Willie's daughter were close friends.

When Steph came to the table, Willie asked when the poster had gone up. Steph said it had been there for well over a year. Steph related that the restaurant business was a really tough market. Steph had gotten into it several years ago when the previous owner had gotten into financial trouble and had to bail.

At first, Steph related, it was a "kick" owning your own show. Friends came in for the "grand opening," and it was a real ego trip. But then things had settled down, and the real chore of competing had settled in. Steph had gotten discouraged at one point, and had gone over to talk with her dad (a long-time Wiggly Lawn Ornaments Inc. employee). Her dad had been sent to a course by Wiggly, and had brought back some material about strategic planning and implementation. He had given it to Steph saying, "See if this helps."

While it was designed for "big business," the principles ought to be the same, and Steph went back to the Armadillo and went through the whole process. Steph said the process worked. Her business was better than ever (Willie had noticed there was always a wait for a seat). Not only that, she was now selling some of the "Dillo's Secret Sauces" through the same mega retailer Wiggly Lawn Ornaments Inc. was using; and . . . she was currently working with several investors about going into franchising.

All Willie could say was thanks. He was dumbfounded by the revelation that material from a course he was sending Wiggly Lawn Ornaments Inc.'s employees to have been used so effectively ("right under his nose") at a local restaurant. Willie quickly finished his lunch and headed back to the office with a mission. First, Wiggly Lawn Ornaments Inc. was going to have a *vision* that meant something. Second, Willie was going to round up everyone who had gone to that course (starting with Steph's dad) and have them help him get this going. If a *vision* worked for the Armadillo Grill, it would surely work for Wiggly.

## "A dead PIG?!?"

It didn't take long for Willie to learn that without ever clearly declaring where it was the company needed to go, and what Wiggly Lawn Ornaments Inc. needed to be and do when it got there, that no one had a very good idea about what to do (beyond what was on the "table" that day). Willie also realized that, without that direction, as the saying goes, "Any path will do," and, as he thought more about it, Wiggly looked more like the story of the Pig and the Fleas. He and others had thought of themselves as "captains" of this "magnificent ship" when, in fact, they were fleas riding on a dead, bloating pig drowned in the river, and "cruising" to wherever the river was taking the carcass. In fact, they weren't piloting Wiggly's ship. They were really only along for the ride.

With that profound insight, Willie went through a short grieving process of denial, then anger, negotiation, and finally acceptance; he came out of it with a serious resolve. The legacy Willie would leave Wiggly Lawn Ornaments Inc. was not of a dead pig floating out of control on a flooded river, but rather of a truly remarkable ship, under power and continuing to successfully navigate through a turbulent, competitive sea. Willie had encountered his first *perception shift*. With that, Willie and Wiggly Lawn Ornaments Inc. went to work, and the self-discovery and learning process began.

There were a myriad of "strategic" decisions that would have to be made right up front. Willie was as action-oriented as they come. He really wanted to get around to "doing something," but the profound self-revelation of his "magnificent ship" and his past role caused him to discipline himself and the others in the organization to put the time in and get it, this "strategic stuff," right the first time. He knew that a good beginning would cut down, if not eliminate, a lot of false starts and recycle, and ultimately lead to a good outcome.

Wiggly Lawn Ornaments Inc. and its three primary suppliers had all been sucked into the same trap of success. All had experienced varying degrees of success, and all had been on their "own journeys," defined, for the most part, by their past history. The problem was that the current state that was emerging was not anything like their past history, and the future state they were moving toward would not resemble their past, and most likely would not even resemble their present. All four of these companies' leaders were being confronted by the same demand, which was for them to lead. Each of the four company's constituents (stakeholders) were looking for their leadership to clearly articulate a direction, provide the motivation and order for the new journey, and keep watch over each transformation, making corrections along the way.

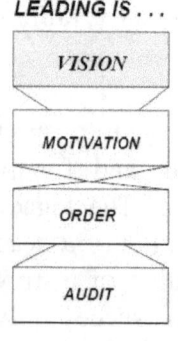

LEADING IS . . .

### *Power up the "PIG"*

The act of leading has four critical elements depicted here. Leading is significantly different than managing (directing with skill) and bossing (do what I tell you to do). While managing and bossing have been much discussed, and factually have been the source of many successes and are not truly the "source of all evil" as some might portray, in a rapidly-paced and continually-changing competitive environment, they really can't hold a candle against leading. There are certain things that can only be accomplished through leading, and change is one of them. Change can't be bossed or managed into an organization. What some discover, when trying these other two approaches, is that the best they get is "compliance to me" when the boss or manager is within "sight." But, when out of sight, the organization reverts to where they have come from. Because of this, the effectiveness of managing and bossing is limited by an individual's scope of endeavor and competency. The larger the scope, the more demanding it is on the individual to "stay in sight." And, if the scope continues to grow beyond the competency of the individual, the situation ultimately swallows up the boss or the manager. This is not the case with people who choose to lead.

Leading is first about establishing a **vision**. A vision is a statement of *ambition*. It defines that ambition in terms that can be internalized, understood, and, more importantly, believed by those being led. If the vision, the statement of ambition, can't be understood and internalized, what is it? Many vision statements resemble the old definition of a camel (a Triple Crown racehorse designed by a committee). Every part is so hedged or wordsmithed that the final statement of ambition is confusing and sometimes contradictory, and it is ultimately ignored.

Some are so cliché they are uniformly ignored or, worse yet, ridiculed by those for whom they were written to inspire (e.g. how many vision statements are there that don't aspire to be "# 1"). I've yet to run across a vision statement that declares: "We want to be a solid # 2." Vision statements that go beyond the mental stretch of an organization can be demotivating. The most common problem is trying to craft a "vision for the ages." It goes beyond mental stretch and results in "mental breakdown."

## Share the Load

The second element of leading is Motivation. Motivation is not something that is externally generated. It is an internal thing. Just like accountability is externally given, responsibility is something that comes from within. Motivation, as with responsibility, comes from within each person. **Motivation** is very simply the *transfer of ownership* from the leader to those that are being led. Motivating is not "cheerleading." It is also not manipulation, and it is definitely not intimidation. Motivating is not a one-time pep talk.

Motivating is a continuum of communication which moves through individual awareness to shared awareness, to individual aims to shared aims, and finally to a shared action. This core process is what enables teaming. A team is a group of individuals who share the same *common aim*, and who: a) See their own *personal success* being accomplished through the *team accomplishing its aims*; and b) See *each team member as needed* if the common aim is to be accomplished. Committees, groups, etc. are differentiated from teams in that one or both of those requisites are missing. The omission of this element alone, failing to establish ownership outside of oneself, is the most frequent error of those that try to lead.

## *Let them go.*

The third element of leading is providing a framework of **order** through which an organization can, in relative safety and with some degree of assurance, make the journey of change (getting across the crevice). *Order* in the case of change or improvement is most aptly defined as ***freedom without chaos***. Order is about the discipline of planning and execution. Order is the orchestration of an organization's efforts and the enabling of critical resources. Organizations always have more on their plates than they have resources to deploy. Order is about establishing a framework that is effective in dealing with these competing needs.

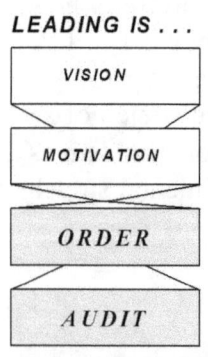

One of the requisites of a team is that every person is needed. That being true, how can the team take the field and be effective if one or more members are "not available?" Many improvement initiatives die or languish because leadership has said *yes* to *too many* things. Failing to make a tough decision (a decision when saying yes to something means saying no to other things which are also desirable) inevitably leads to chaos. What is truly disappointing is when the leader has clearly articulated the vision and gone through the hard work of establishing a shared ownership, but then fails to provide the order to move forward. Organizational wheel spinning (expenditures of effort without progress) leads to organizational burnout. Success and progress are the fuels for continued success and progress. Without order there won't be much, if any, progress or success; and without that . . .

The fourth and final element of leading is **audit**. Auditing is not about "checking back" in a year to see how it is going. Auditing is about the continual **observation and comparison** of what is happening versus the plan (order) and expectations that have been delivered. In a change or improvement situation, auditing needs to be driven by *facts* vs. *perceptions*. Perceptions are getting in touch with your feelings; facts are dealing with the truth.

## *Mom wouldn't be pleased.*

Let's go back and take a look at the behavior of Joe "BA" Hurang, CEO of Higgles Power Zone Inc. "Old Joe" really tried hard to deliver a vision. Even though what he said was, to a great degree, cliché and trite, most of the Higgles people had already felt the need for what Joe was saying. So give "old Joe" a C for Vision. With regard to motivation, Jim Spin (with Joe's concurrence), had laid nothing out beyond the "event" of the rally that would allow the organization to go through the process of internalizing and reconciling what Joe had said, which would lead them to ownership and a shared path forward. The result was a flattening of the "culture curve." So "old Joe" gets a D for Motivation because some did try to act, and there were pockets of ownership. But, these same pockets of ownership resulted in a combative and adversarial relationship within Higgles that cannot be

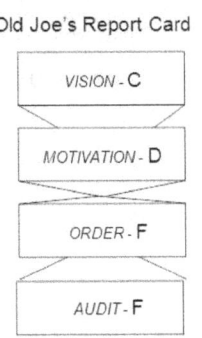

Old Joe's Report Card

VISION - C

MOTIVATION - D

ORDER - F

AUDIT - F

described as anything less than chaos. So, "old Joe" gets an F for order. Regarding audit, "old Joe" never gave it a thought. He was still under the impression that, if he said it, it would be done. It was only after some time had passed, and the newly-recruited MBA's competitive survey results were in that Joe came to realize that something wasn't right. "Old Joe" gets another F.

Both Joe and Willie were up against the same wall. Both were confronting environments in which not only the rules had changed, but the scoreboard and scoring had changed as well. What made it worse was that the skills that had gotten each to where they were today weren't going to give them the future they wanted, and might in fact prove to be the strongest restraining force pushing back against improvement: their own personal inability to change themselves.

The only way out of this mess was for both Joe and Willie (and ultimately every person in their companies) to deal first with their individual resistance to change, and then collectively, as a company, deal with it, through the process of clearly stating what the company needs to be and do through defining and communicating an understandable Vision statement. Fear is fuel for resistance, and there is no more powerful source of fear than the "unknown." A Vision statement can either clear away the cloud of mystery or it can make that cloud darker and more ominous. A Vision is as integral to a company as a Vision is integral to leading.

Effective Visions draw a line in the sand, pound a stake in the ground about the Values, Offerings, and Segments the company aspires to serve, not only its customers and markets, but also its ownership, its people, and its communities. This defines what it wants to be and do, and how it defines success. It is only in this context that individuals and organizations can begin to identify their individual and collective resistance and fears.

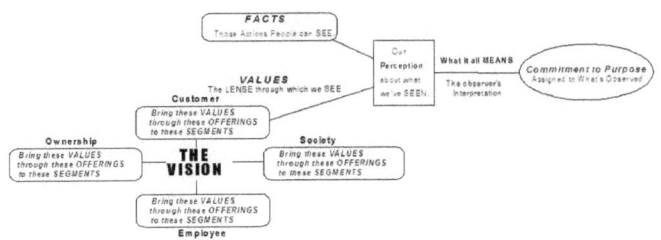

There really isn't any "formula" or prescription for a perfect Vision. It is hard, strategic work. Tactical errors cost money. Strategic errors cost the "business." VISION statements are strategic! Yet, so many times, organizations rush through this, looking at the "end" as a document, versus the "end" as being a STRATEGIC BEGINING. Vision statements are the highest form of organizational decision making.

## *The journey begins.*

Let's go back to Wiggly Lawn Ornaments Inc.'s attempt to "transform" from the figurative dead pig to a magnificent ship. Willie (founder and CEO) had undergone what some psychologists might call "a significant emotional event." He'd experienced a profound insight that had gone to the core, altering forever his business "genetic code." From that day on, this experience would affect every facet of his "business behavior." With Willie at the "helm," and a lot of patience, Willie was able to lead his direct reports through the same discovery process he'd experienced; what once went unrecognized was now very "visible" to all. They had all experienced the same "genetic altering." The Wiggly "Leadership Team" was born, and it was now ready to get down to the hard work of being strategic. They shared the same feelings about what had to get done; they all knew that each of their personal futures depended on getting it done. They collectively grasped the realization that they all needed each other if they were to "get this done."

Everyone was already "too busy," and there didn't seem to be any time left in the day. Willie talked it through. They all concluded that staff meetings were pretty much a waste of time. As somebody bravely said, "It's about regurgitating what we already know." Another drew the analogy of a bunch of elephants sitting around for hours trumpeting to one another. So, for now, the time once allocated for staff meetings would be devoted solely to doing the "strategic work" of defining what it was the company was going to be and do for the four Wiggly Lawn Ornaments Inc. stakeholders that would define Wiggly's future success. It was a beginning . . . and often the most difficult part of a journey is getting started.

## *"What we have here is a failure to communicate!"*

After the first couple of meetings, during which they seemed to be going in circles (nothing new), Willie went back to the "charm school" stuff they'd collected and shared, and came across a principle that said "all work is a process." It said that meetings ought to have inputs, "a transform," outputs, and results. Well, that made sense. He also found a "process map." Willie had always assumed that communication was a matter of someone speaking and someone listening. But this went a lot further, and Willie concluded that what the Wiggly Lawn Ornaments Inc. staff had been doing was taking turns talking, but, instead of listening, everyone was politely being silent, waiting for their turn to talk.

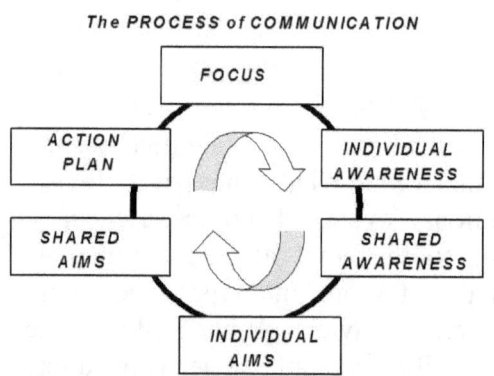

So, Willie brought the process map back to the team (pictured here) and began using it. The way it worked was that each meeting would have an *Aim*, an agenda with time limits, and a desired output (in terms of products and results). That provided focus. Everybody made a commitment to prepare, and they were usually ready with their inputs when they got to the meeting. As long as they stayed with this process, they usually got what they needed. It was a "pain" at first. It was hard work to "listen" as each disclosed their Individual Awareness about the meeting content, and equally difficult to converge that to Shared Awareness, a composite of Facts and Perceptions, they could all agree to. But, it really began to pay off. They found that "recycle" (going back over the same old stuff meeting after meeting) was nearly eliminated. They also found themselves beginning to be perceived by the Wiggly Lawn Ornaments Inc. organization as a "team" because they were all talking the same "story."

There always seemed to be someone (Willie more times than not) who wanted to leap ahead to action, but the discipline of staying with the process always paid off. Listening to what each manager wanted to accomplish (Individual Aims) after they had reached a consensus around a Shared Awareness, and then converging on a Shared Aim nearly eliminated the nefarious "hidden agenda syndrome" that they collectively discovered had been "eating their lunch" in the past. The action plan after each meeting never resembled anyone's personal idea about what it should be coming into the meeting, and they all agreed at the end of each meeting that the output was better than anyone could have thought of by themselves. The more success they had in having an orderly, efficient, and productive meeting, the more trust and expertise they developed in the "process." But, more importantly, everybody owned the action plan and worked harder to be ready for the next session. Willie mused that maybe this was what "consensus" building was all about.

### *Values/Offerings/Segments*

After a month of work (they had quickly expanded their available time for this task) Wiggly's Leadership Team had hammered out a vision statement. It systematically addressed serving each of the stakeholder's needs and wants by making the fundamental decisions around the *Value* Wiggly Lawn Ornaments Inc. would be to each of them; the *Offerings* (the "vehicles" that would deliver that value); and the *Segments* (or, better put, who's in and who's out) that they would serve. When it was done, what surprised them all was that it *made sense,* and that Wiggly Lawn Ornaments Inc. serving one stakeholder actually served the others.

They discovered a reciprocal nature among the stakeholders. One stakeholder couldn't be successful without all the others being successful. They had defined their future success in a highly-competitive and demanding environment they sensed was coming.

It really felt good. But, as they looked at it (and indeed it was a great piece of work), they realized that they had only declared **what** they aspired to become . . . not **how** they were going to do it. Many organizations make the mistake of stopping here. It's easy to do. Coming up with a statement of Vision (one that makes sense) is hard enough work, but figuring out how to get there is an order of magnitude more difficult. Willie and the Leadership Team felt drained. None could remember the last time they had worked this hard. They had all been creatures of habit; they had been on "cruise control" for a long time. The afterglow of their immediate accomplishment was quickly dampened by the recognition that they'd only completed the first step. The fact that they had completed it, though, gave them all a sense of confidence that they were going to succeed, and that was something they really hadn't felt for a while. They were on their way.

# CHAPTER III

## AFTER the VISION
## "WHAT to be STRATEGIC ABOUT"

There always seems to be a mental struggle within organizations as to what exactly it is they mean when they use the word STRATEGY. There is significant time and energy wasted debating whether a proposal is a strategy, a vision, a tactic, a mission, or a plan. This is time and energy that ought to be spent on "content," versus "pigeon holing." The struggle, and the inherent loss of speed and energy, exists because organizations fail to come to a Shared Awareness about not only the definition of the word Strategy, but also, and sometimes more significantly, a Shared Awareness about the context in which the word is being used. This lack of a "common language" often persists indefinitely without resolution.

In a business context, the word strategy or strategic is as likely to be used when describing making a sales call as it is when talking about entering a new market, or about developing a new offering. The truth is that, in a given context, any or all of these can be a strategy or described as strategic. The word strategy has military roots. **Strategy** is derived from the Greek word *strategia*, meaning generalship, or, more to the point, the *work of a general*. Strategy is about making choices, specifically choices in a military context, which are reserved for and made by those with the *rank* of general. The definitions of strategy include: 1) the science and art of employing the political, economic, psychological, and military forces of a nation or group of nations to afford the maximum support to adopted policies in peace and war; and, 2) the science and art of military command exercised to meet the enemy in combat under advantageous conditions. For illustration, the *Vision* of the Allies in World War II against the Axis forces was, simply put, to *win the war*.

**WORLD WAR II ALLIED VISION**
*WIN the WAR*

**ALLIED GLOBAL STRATEGY**
Win in Europe FIRST        Win in ASIA SECOND

European Theater STRATEGY
Air Supremacy
Plans & Tactics        Ground Invasion
                       Plans & Tactics

The *strategy* developed for the global conflict was to *win first in Europe*. From this strategy, other local theater strategies cascaded, all still the *work of the generals*. What was changing as these choices cascaded down was a decreasing scope of what to be strategic about. The work of generals was not solely confined to simply making the choice to win the war in Europe first. There were a myriad of choices that the generals involved made around increasingly smaller scopes of endeavor before their staff could effectively begin the planning, staffing, and then, the implementation process. This myriad of choices, when cascaded and linked together, became the Allied Strategic Plan.

A second parallel illustration of strategy is the Persian Gulf War. A vastly smaller "scope" of endeavor to begin with dramatically changed the *work of the generals* (compared to WWII). In the context of World War II, the Gulf Conflict might have easily been described as a plan or a tactic, delegated and carried out by staff groups, by people holding less than the rank of "general." But is that to say that the work of the generals in the Gulf Conflict was not strategic or that

**Persian Gulf War ALLIED VISION**
*Stability in the Middle East*

**ALLIED "GLOBAL" STRATEGY**
Political Intervention FIRST        Military Intervention SECOND

Political & Economic STRATEGY        Military Theater STRATEGY
Trade Blockade    Sanctions          Air Supremacy
Plans & Tactics   Plans & Tactics    Plans & Tactics        Ground Invasion
                                                            Plans & Tactics

those who made the choices about the African Campaign in WWII were not acting equally as strategic as the generals of the Gulf War were? Of course not.

People will invalidly claim that the "work of the generals" in a business organization is confined only to those of the highest rank and position. The truth is that there are "generals" functioning everywhere within an organization, depending on the context and scope of work. Taking World War II as the standard by which the "work of the general" would be compared forever more would be nonsensical. The work of the general changes as the scope and context of what to be strategic about changes, as does who is functioning in a role of *generalship*. The same is true in a business organization.

## *Is this a strategy, tactic, plan, mission, or what?*

*Strategy* can be further understood in the context of the words that most frequently surround it -- tactics, plans, and missions. A tactic is defined as a method of employing forces in combat, a device for accomplishing an end. Tactics have an action level orientation. Winning in Europe is not really what anyone would call "action level." Seizing a town or city in Europe during WWII is. In a business context, a *strategy* might be Market ABC Share Leadership. A *tactic* would be to win 100% share at Customer XYZ. Share Leadership isn't very actionable, i.e. something an organization can immediately sink its teeth into and go out and do. On the other hand, getting 100% share at a certain customer account is.

A *plan* is the blueprint of engagement (in a military context). It is the ordered, sequential, and interconnected parallel linkage of choices that, if successfully implemented, will result in the desired outcome. A plan addresses efficiency and deployment of effort. It is the linking and rationalizing of an array of interdependent actions.

Without this "order," there would be chaos, or, maybe worse, no action. The best way to visualize this is what is commonly referred to as a network plan or "Critical Path," shown here.

## THE PLAN

MISSION -- "The REASON we're out here doing this?"

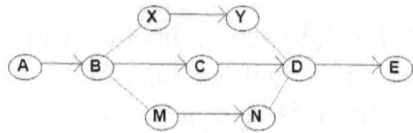

Tactics -- AB, BC, CD, DE, MN, XY
AB must be complete before BC, XY, and MN can be started
BC must be complete before CD can be started
DE cannot be started until MN, CD, and XY are complete
Completing DE ends the Mission

Plans are not confined to *either* strategies *or* tactics, but rather, apply to both. Strategic plans are the cascading of strategy that, when carried out, will accomplish "the vision." Tactical plans are the cascading of tactics that, when carried out, will accomplish a strategy. How the two differ from each other can best be thought of in terms of outcomes. The stake of a strategic plan is victory or defeat. The stake of a tactical plan is progress or setback. Sometimes terms like "below the waterline" and "above the waterline" are used to help organizations visualize the difference.

*Mission* is a word that is most often confused with Vision. Strictly defined, Mission is the *act or instance of sending*. In a broader sense, it *defines why and gives broad guidance to someone going "out there"* to try to do something. Just as with plans, there can be Strategic Missions and Tactical Missions. A Mission begins with the definition and *application* of resources to a strategy or a tactic. It ends when the strategy or tactic has been completed, or when the strategy or tactic is changed or removed by the organization. Mission describes the reasoning behind the actual deployment of resources (people, money, time, etc.). Mission statements have timelines that are either on the "horizon" or closer at hand. Vision statements are always "over the horizon." Mission statements include answers to *What*, *How*, and *Why* an individual, or more often a team, is working to accomplish an end (whether that end is tactical or strategic).

Under a **"Corporate Vision,"** a **Strategy** might be *Market ABC Share Leadership*. Under that strategy's umbrella would be a

***Tactic*** of *Acquiring 100% share at Customer XYZ*. A tactical plan would include all the blocks of work that have to be successfully completed to achieve 100% share at XYZ. A ***Tactical Mission*** statement for the plan might be . . .

*"Capture 100% share at Customer XYZ by m/d/y (what) in a way that builds credibility around our value to customers and our integrity and commitment to our customer's plans (how) so that this experience can be quickly leveraged to other customers and accounts (why)."*

A complimentary ***Strategic Mission*** statement might be . . .
*"To grow annual sales by 50% within 24 months (what) in a way that secures industry standing and leverages our existing assets (how) so that we gain experience and focus on securing the future we have defined for our stakeholders (why)."*

In many instances, when an organization finally "breaks the code" and arrives at a shared awareness around a common language through which they can communicate, there is often a period of short-lived, euphoric relief that ends with the thought . . . NOW WHAT! Some begin the task of trying to "pigeon hole" all the things they already share some degree of consensus around under the proper headings. It isn't all bad, unless that's all they do. The core question is WHAT DO WE NEED TO BE STRATEGIC ABOUT?

## "The Tormenting Triad & the Feisty Five"

First, an organization's leadership needs to revisit their Vision. The *vision* defines success in terms of an organization's four primary stakeholders. The context in which that success is defined is the leadership's image of a **future state** context, within which their organization will exist. That context can be thought of in terms of the triadic relationship among **Customers/Markets**, **Competitors**, and **Environments** that is illustrated here. A fairly common misadventure in strategic thinking is the assumption that this context is static. In fact, it is a very dynamic relationship, with each of the three driving changes, responses, and reconciliation by the others. For example, a change in the environment in which the customers and/or competitors exist, which could be due to virtually anything, from a governmental regulation, to an economic cycle, to a cultural evolution by consumers or societies to new levels of expectation, might drive a response by existing customers and markets. That, in turn, would have to be reconciled by the competitors, who supply the customers, who provide the end product or service. Some common themes of environmental shifts

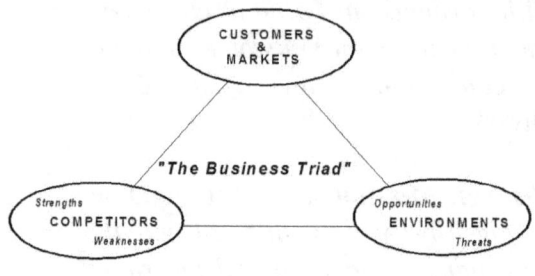

are *lightness*, which has impacted every form of hard goods, from automobiles to power tools. *Portability* has driven changes and reconciliation from telecommunications, to health care, to retirement benefits. Government regulation on pollution abatement is an ongoing dynamic. A competitive innovation, an entry by a new competitor or customer, the development of a substitute, etc. are all examples of activators which continue to fuel this dynamic. This triad and dynamic exist in every enterprise, from education to heavy industry.

A second leadership mishap is to linearly extrapolate the present to the future, assuming that the only dynamics involved are bigger and more. The life cycles of products and services have dramatically decreased. To think that an organization will be providing substantially the same product or service forever more to an ever-growing field of consumers, with essentially the same competitors competing in essentially the same way, is a "strategic mistake." So, the first thing any organization needs to be strategic about is the FUTURE. That being said, *how* they engage the future, what areas they need to cascade strategy from, can be boiled down to the five fields of attack pictured here. These five can be subdivided and expanded infinitely.

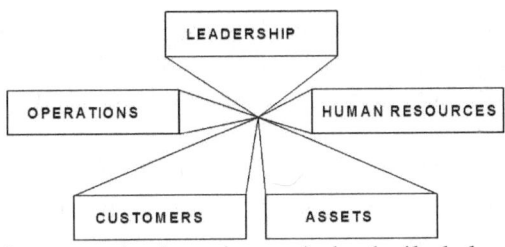

But, this strategic domain can't be boiled down to less than five. All five of these are very much interconnected and interdependent (just as in the preceding triad), and you can't impact or change one without affecting the others, or without the others having to make reconciling shifts.

## *The 500-pound Turkey*

Let's take the case of Haggle Corp. Haggle Corp had been the original supplier for Wiggly Lawn Ornaments Inc., and they had both more or less started doing business at about the same time. Haggle Corp had grown a lot bigger and a lot faster than Wiggly Lawn Ornaments Inc., but they had still managed to keep their company private and in the family's hands. The company oozed the values and beliefs of its founder, Harry Huckster. Harry was the classic boss. He had been there when the first brick was laid, and while every piece of equipment was installed. He knew how everything ought to be done, and he was not hesitant to "get people in line." Harry had also felt the presence and impact of Arlans General Corp.'s entry into the market on Haggle's revenue stream, and Harry was concerned. Arlans was beginning to show up at other accounts beyond Wiggly Lawn Ornaments Inc. (no lost sales yet). Harry was also an astute observer of Higgles Power Zone (which had started up only a couple of years after Haggle Corp. was founded), and Harry was equally confused as to exactly what it was that Higgles was doing over there. Some days the stories and rumors concerned him; other days they gave him a good night's sleep.

A couple of years back, Harry had decided that he was tired of "doing all the work," and that other people needed to "pick up" some of the load. He hadn't figured out yet that for other people to "pick up the work," Harry would have to *stop doing the work*.

Regardless, after a series of terminations, and Harry continually trying to bring in new people who'd "pick up the work" (to no avail), Harry happened to meet O.E. Pickens, an HR specialist.

In a conversation on an airplane, O.E. had impressed on Harry that the answer to his quandary was right under his nose. All Harry had to do was develop the skills and capabilities of the people who were already there. O.E. told Harry that it's a higher-leveraged deal to train a loyal employee to do "new things" than it is to hire a person already capable of doing "new things" and develop them to be a loyal employee. This made sense to Harry. One thing led to another, and three months later O.E. Pickens was the new VP of HR for Haggle Corp. (you don't even want to know what happened to the old VP).

O.E. hit the ground running, developing an array of new training programs for everything from specific skills, to computer literacy, to basic team training. Along with the programs, O.E. hired a cadre of skilled HR professionals capable of developing and delivering the training for the needed skills to do "new things." Harry noticed O.E.'s presence on the daily cost reports (his price was five grand a day), but, Harry reflected, this was the price of progress. About six months into it, O.E. went in to see Harry to say that there was a problem. Harry's antennae were already up, so he interjected quickly that he had a problem too. Harry had spent a lot of money by then, and the only thing O.E.'s programs seemed to be doing was trashing the bottom line. Harry's complaint was, in a phrase . . . "Show me the money!"

O.E. replied that that's why he was there. People were now ready and able to start "picking up the work." The problem was that Harry needed to change his leadership style. The employees needed to be delegated the authority to get on with it. Harry was perplexed, asking what authority it exactly was that they wanted delegated. After a long discussion, Harry abruptly ended it. Harry said that "they" have the ". . . authority to ask my permission," and that he would block out a two-hour time slot on alternate Thursdays ("unless something comes up") to be available for people to come in and review what they wanted to do so he could grant them permission.

After three "visits to the king" (as the alternate Thursday meetings quickly became dubbed), O.E. was quick on the uptake, and reluctantly recognized an impenetrable wall for what it was. Each visit ended with Harry requesting more information before he was willing to go along with the requests that came in. Harry prided himself on being able to ask "good" questions, and these meetings were a venue in which this talent really flourished. Harry was quickly mastering paralysis by analysis. Two months later, O.E. jumped ship, leaving behind a super training staff, a big bill, and an organization full of newly-trained and very frustrated people, all chanting in unison . . . "I told you so." What Harry failed to realize is that if you develop capabilities for which there are no outlets, it's not going to end well. In this case, Harry had spent money and developed human resource capabilities without making adjustments to the Leadership or Operations in order to be able to absorb, use, and leverage them. It's analogous to buying a loaf of Texas Toast and not buying a wide mouth toaster, or genetically breeding a 500-pound turkey for retail sales. What's the point?

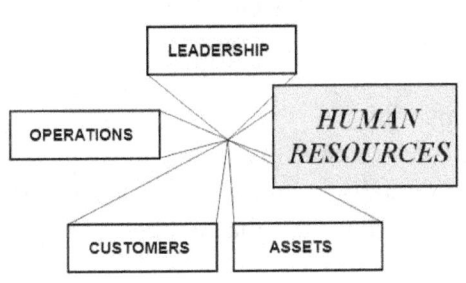

## *Does anyone know how to turn this thing on?*

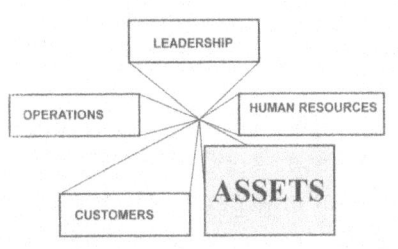

Over at Higgles Power Zone, Joe "BA" Hurang was running into a similar problem. *Assets* were overrunning *Human Resources*. In "BA's" case, he'd been born again on a lot of fronts, and had gone ahead and authorized the total renovation of one of the plants, investing heavily in automation. "BA" had only heard a part of the message -- a 60% reduction in equipment operators, and a 200% increase in capability. Old "BA" had really been singing the praises of automation on the cocktail circuit ("BA" wasn't a wine and cheese sort of dude). What "BA" had missed in the project discussions, however, was that for every 2 equipment operators Higgles was able to excise, Higgles would either have to train or hire an electrical and instrument mechanic, a mechanical robotics technician, and a computer code masher *(+3 −2 = +1)*.

The second weekend after the "factory reps" from the equipment suppliers left, the whole plant went down, and no one remaining had a clue as to how to get it going again. The new equipment and automation had greatly increased capability. What hadn't changed was the capability of the human resources to maintain and operate this new equipment (as a matter of fact, the human resource capability had actually been reduced because "BA" had been quick to permanently lay off the excess equipment operators).

To make matters worse, by Tuesday morning Higgles Power Zone Inc. had fallen behind on deliveries, and their first customer had shut down (but "BA" was still pretty good at dealing with the "dreaded customer"). One thing that decreased Higgles' ability to get their arms around the true "disaster" (Higgles would discover that two weeks later) was that, on that same weekend, Higgles had also installed a new, automated phone system (that had allowed "BA" to layoff the Higgles receptionist, along with about 20% of the sales support staff). On Tuesday morning, when shit started hitting the fan in the customers' shops, in order to make phone contact with Higgles, a customer now needed to navigate through three, computer-voice-generated menus before they got their first chance to speak with a real person. But, even then, there was less than a 30% chance that the caller would not be dumped into the voice mail system and be faced with another two menus to conquer before they got a chance to speak. Only a few stayed with the phone system long enough to leave behind a profound and profane comment for those Higgles folks to find a week later, after they had all been trained on how to access their voice mail accounts. There were more than a few cracked phone handsets at Higgles customers' shops in the weeks that followed. This was a second case of assets out of alignment with human resources.

## *Doing the right things right in the right order.*

Both Harry Huckster at Haggle Corp. and "BA" Hurang at Higgles Power Zone Inc. had single-handedly built and fired "torpedoes" into their own organizations. In both instances, the torpedoes hit right at the "waterline." Although significantly different in nature, both these events had their roots in a common cause, specifically, tactics before strategy. Neither Harry nor "BA" had done the work of "generalship" that would have uncovered and linked all the "if/then" and "cause/effect" relationships that would have been addressed and dealt with by their staff. Putting tactics before strategy, or strategy before vision, is the root cause of the commonplace phenomena of the "program syndrome" so very prevalent in the business world today. The core issue is **context**. Context gives significance and meaning to that which is being examined or trying to be understood. In the instance of a business organization, the "Business Triad" is the *context* in which the Vision has significance. The Vision becomes the *context* in which the Strategies have significance. And finally, the Strategies are the *context* in which Tactics take on significance and meaning. In the absence of this cascaded thinking, anything is possible. *Context* falls under the ownership of an organization's leadership -- its "generalship." Providing this kind of **context** to an organization enables the freedom within the organization to deliberately move forward, and with speed.

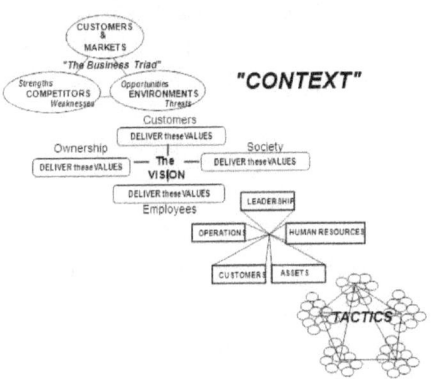

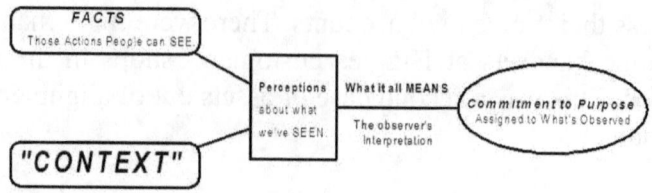

**Who's going to provide it?**

This complete *Context* makes up the lenses for the organization to view what is happening, and place value on it and show commitment to it. Regardless, someone will always provide a *context* if the leadership does not. More typically, many context advocates will emerge inside of and outside of organizations, trying to advance their own parochial interests. This one aspect of leadership, providing *context*, is central to success, whether it is on a strategic or tactical level.

## *An organization is its people.*

Getting back to the five strategic fields of endeavor, **Human Resources** is the area that is seemingly most straightforward, yet most often muddled in the strategic thinking process.

The muddling arises from the fact that the "generalship" has to make the choice of whether their human resources are an *asset* or a *cost*. In the highly-competitive business environment that exists today, there is a significant body of evidence that supports the premise that human resources are not only an asset, but are also the only asset of an organization that has the ability to *appreciate*, or increase in value, over time. An organization's people are the only sustainable competitive advantage. Technology, equipment, etc. all *depreciate* and lose value over time, and must be strategically and tactically dealt with on a renewal basis.

The appreciation process of human resources comes from the fact that the cumulative experience of people is additive, versus the fact that the cumulative use of equipment subtracts (because of wear & tear) from the equipment's continuing viability. The knowledge acquired by people through experience builds and expands non-linearly. To say that it is an either/or situation, that human resources are either an asset or a cost, is not correct either. The work of an organization's generalship is to determine which elements of their human resources are assets, and which are costs, and then to develop strategies and plans of action accordingly.

Years ago, most companies (regardless of what business they were in) looked at computer programmers and analysts as an asset. With the advent of companies whose core competency and business is software and software development, most of the companies (whose business is other than computer software) have shed their "computer" people and moved that facet of human resources from the asset column to the cost column. The answer again lies in cumulative experience. A person in a software company is going to accumulate experience faster, and thereby appreciate faster in that environment, than a counterpart in a business whose core competency and endeavor is not software. There is no contest when it comes to who is going to outperform whom.

This sort of diligence around human resource strategies has to be accomplished in concert and in synergy with strategies developed and acted on in the four other fields. "BA" at Higgles Power Zone Inc. got his organization jammed up when the human resource capability got behind the maintenance and operational requirements of the new equipment. If an organization doesn't raise the human resource capability at the same rate as equipment and technology demands increase, it will get in trouble every time.

## Concrete Feet

The next strategic field of endeavor is **assets**. A lot of time and energy is spent by most organizations in this field. It includes not only the bricks, steel, and equipment, but also the inventories and working capital of business organizations. In addition, such things as technology, patents, rights, and all "raw materials" that are purchased from outside of the company's business are a part of it. This is definitely a field where *renewal* is the byword. Each one of the five strategic fields is make/break, but this is one area where generally the least amount of flexibility exists once the die is cast. Strategic decisions about assets tend to lock organizations in because of their cost and permanency. Decisions about the technological path an organization will go down, the physical buildings and equipment, supplier alliances, etc. are difficult and costly to undo once made. The concept of "flexibility" isn't the total cure either. There is still a significant degree of inflexibility. If you lock into metal forming equipment (flexible or not) and the customers and markets swing to composites or plastics, an organization is sitting on a huge amount of "cash" that has, overnight, depreciated to zero. Because of the inherent longer timelines in this field, and the inherent degree of intractableness, this field is the source of many "below the waterline" hits. Strategic decisions in the field of assets are, in many ways, like putting your feet in concrete. Any organization, whether it is service or manufacturing-based, has to take careful aim when they pick their asset strategies. These choices can't be undone quickly once they are put in motion.

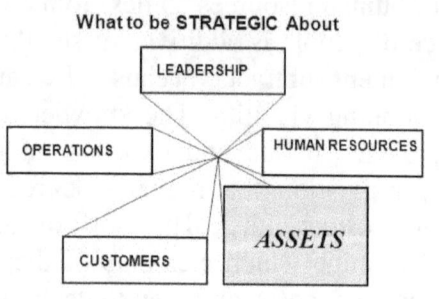

### "Whither?"

This leads to the third field of strategy, **customers** and **markets**. This is the field that ultimately leads and aims the organization. Many a company has been lost because they failed to understand, or understood but failed to develop or implement, correct strategy. There have been countless startup entrepreneurial companies that bet the farm and lost because they failed to properly gauge the value of their offerings. It goes both ways. Some completely missed the target, which resulted in no demand. Others hit the target so squarely dead center that the demand growth rapidly overran their assets, operations, human resources, and leadership. They were either forced to sell out, or allowed the advantage of being the first in the market to slip away, opening the door to more agile competition. Understanding where your present and future competencies will have value and what the needs and wants of those market segments and customers are and will be is paramount. Yet, many organizations get caught up in the success of the present. That lulls them into complacency, and they find themselves another case study for some business school review. They just weren't paying attention and evolving their market and customer strategies in concert with what was really going on out there.

## "Yeah but!"

The fourth strategic field is *operations*. Operations, without a doubt, is the most frequent "whipping boy" or the one found guilty of being the "tail that wags the dog" of any of the five. Whereas **customers** lead, **operations** follow. Operations are dependent on not only what plays out in the customer field, but also on assets and human resources. It is a universal fact that organizations are continually lamenting the fact that they can always sell what

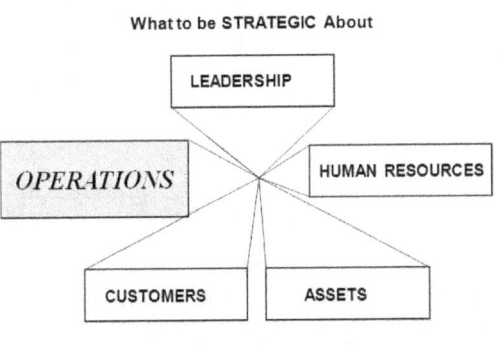

operations can't deliver. Much of this is politics, or artfully playing the game of "who's to blame." Operations are where the bulk of the value-adding activity of an organization takes place. Operations is the process and supporting structure for the "create, sell, make, deliver" value chain. The fact of the matter is that strategies for operations, which should ideally be made and realized "just-in-time," often don't get thought about until the organization is raising their heads, trying to catch the license plate number of the 18-wheeler that just flattened them.

Organizations as a whole don't plan for success. They play with a psychology of hoping to win versus one of expecting to win. In the former instance, changes in human resources and assets, and strategic improvements in operations aren't made until <u>well after</u> they are needed. In the latter case, organizations plan for success, and capability is ready and waiting when and if opportunity knocks. The issue and barrier is the risk.

## *<u>The Rifling in the Barrel</u>*

Strategy is fundamentally about risk management. There are two sides to risk management: the risk of success, and the risk of failure. Who owns risk management and develops processes to effectively deal with it is the fifth strategic field – ***leadership***. This is the overall guidance and steering system of an organization. Leadership aims the organization and guides it – like the rifling in the barrel of a gun. Poor leadership is the proverbial shotgun approach – it hits a lot of places and it may or may not make an impact.

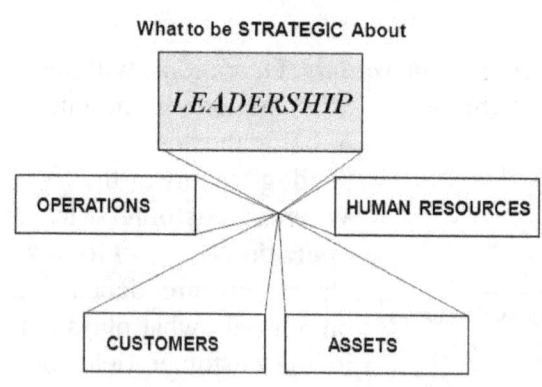

The leadership process is the systematic way in which organizations take in data, transform data into information, combine informational streams into knowledge, and act on it.

If you ask most organizations to show you their leadership process, they will very quickly flip out an organization chart. Organization charts aren't process. They are the structure that enables (or in many instances disables) the leadership process. In the case of Haggle Corp., *Harry Huckster was the **process***. Forget what the organization chart looked like; that structure was there to do Harry's bidding. In the case of Willie at Willie's Wiggly Lawn Ornaments, Willie had just discovered the need for a leadership process. Willie was moving from a state where he had been the process to a leadership process of systematic and cascaded thinking that continually engaged those in the organization who could have the most *impact* through what *they knew*, not necessarily the position they held. Joe "BA" Hurang at Higgles Power Zone had inadvertently thrown out whatever process there had been with the emergence of his "born again" phase. In all three of these cases, it wasn't necessarily the leader who was broken, it was the ***leadership process*** that was broken and in need of an upgrade.

# CHAPTER IV

## The LEADERSHIP PROCESS

*Leadership* is a word that has become so commonplace and overused that it seldom elicits a "thinking" response. It's more likely to go in one ear and out the other. In a dictionary, *leadership* can be found under the definition of *leader*. They are one in the same (according to Webster's). Both are nouns, and both are used to describe a person engaged in the act of leading. Other meanings range from the party elite, to a person with commanding authority, to a person characterized by the extreme use of demagogy, to even a person endowed with heroic or mystical character. Two meanings, buried in this matrix, are simply a ***guide*** or a ***conductor***. These two words can give a wealth of insight into what leadership is through analogy.

It has been reported that the path of creativity always traverses the passage of analogy at some point. The use of analogies is a way to gain a leap in insight and understanding that might not otherwise be possible. The verb form of the word ***guide*** simply means to direct. Synonyms for ***guide*** are ***lead***, ***steer***, ***pilot***, and ***engineer***.

- ***Guide*** alludes to an intimate knowledge of the way, and all its difficulties and dangers.
- ***Lead*** implies going ahead to show the way and keep those who follow in order.
- ***Steer*** refers to a capacity to keep to a chosen course and stresses the ability to maneuver correctly.

- ○ ***Pilot*** suggests guidance over a dangerous, intricate, or complicated course.
- ○ ***Engineer*** implies direction by one who finds ways to avoid or overcome difficulties in achieving an end.
- ○ ***Conductor*** is described as the leader of a musical ensemble.

A conductor is a sharp contrast to a guide. Whereas guide alludes to danger and the demands of adventure and venturing into the unknown, conductor creates a mental picture of bringing disparate noises and sounds together in a way that is pleasing, a harmony and order that is unifying. Compare the experience of a symphony orchestra warming up immediately before a concert to the beauty and synergistic symmetry when the orchestra is placed under the direction of a conductor.

So, when discussing ***leadership***, there ought to be denoted and connoted thinking taking place: thinking about someone who provides an intimate knowledge of the way, and its difficulties and dangers; thinking about someone who is a beacon that keeps those who follow in order; thinking about someone who keeps an organization on a chosen course and enables the ability to maneuver correctly; thinking about someone who is a source of guidance over a dangerous, intricate, or complicated course, someone who finds ways to avoid or overcome difficulties in achieving an end, yet also provides unity and harmony, focus, and effectiveness and efficiency of effort. When you bundle these features, attributes, and qualities of leadership together, and ask the question, "Have you experienced good ***leadership*** lately?" the preponderance response is seldom, and, in some instances, never.

## *"I just don't get it."*

This leads to the question of WHY. Why is there such a perceived absence of leadership? There isn't a lack of people willing and trying, or a lack of circumstances and situations that could benefit from it. The answer lies not in opportunity or willingness, but in the fact that, no matter how you cut it, leadership is very complex work. All work is a process.

Leadership is a process. It has inputs (information, data, and knowledge). It has a transform that takes the inputs, does work on them, and produces an output. That output has a result or impact on the arena where leadership is being directed. If leadership is thought of as a process, it can be improved upon by measuring the qualities of its output and results, and by measuring the reduction and elimination of waste in its transform.

### *The Leadership Process*

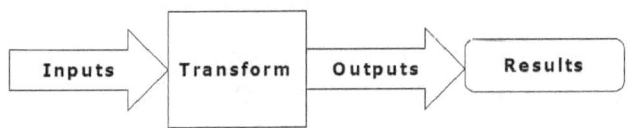

There is a plethora of information, ideas, data, knowledge, etc. in the form of inputs that impact organizations daily. There is a continuum of "raw material" waiting to be transformed into a usable output. There already exists, in every organization, a *leadership process*. If that process were *mapped*, it might end up being a name in some cases (as was the case at Haggle Corp), an event (annual meeting, etc.), or even the person who answers the phone and gives an answer. Or, it might be a systematic, disciplined, well-documented process both in form and function.

The "circle" that is drawn defines the context and content of a leadership process, not the process itself. The circle can be drawn around a corporation, a plant site, a work group, a school, a service center, or even a family. Regardless, there is always a leadership process present, refined or not. What differentiates a mega-company's process from a family unit's leadership process is the scope of work to which leadership is being applied and who is doing the work of leadership. The process is the same, even though it covers substantially different territory and content. A leadership process has three (3) distinct "layers" of activity. The first layer is about making the *choices* about whatever is within "the circle," choices that give direction and meaning. The second is about *planning* around the choices that have been made. That gives a tangible sense of order to the organization. The third activity layer is the carrying out of the plans, the *doing*. Within each of these layers, there are three (3) distinct blocks of work. The first is selecting the *targets*. The second is getting *alignment* around those targets, and the third is the work of *implementation*.

## The PROCESS

The model that follows pictorially maps a leadership work process and the content of each of its pieces in terms of their broad outputs. Each one of these blocks of work has to be further developed into the inputs and process steps that are carried out to produce these outputs.

Each block is distinctive and additive to the others. The output of one becomes the input for another. They are all interdependent and connected. The work of leadership typically flows from the top to bottom and from left to right. But, as facts, information, data, and knowledge are developed; they become inputs, and can feed back into any or all of the work blocks for processing, reconciliation, and action.

Another way of thinking about the three layers of activity portrayed in the three columns is that the DOING column is the daily nuts and bolts of an organization trying to change or improve itself.

**The LEADERSHIP PROCESS**

|  | CHOOSING | PLANNING | DOING |
|---|---|---|---|
| TARGET | What the entity aspires to BE & DO in its future state. | WHAT & WHAT ORDER things need to get done in order to progress toward the future defined. | Determine the changes and lead the shifts that must take place to ensure success. |
| ALIGN | Aligned BEHAVIORAL PRINCIPLES that will guide it. | Aligned PLANS that can be acted on that provide order. | Aligned EFFORT. |
| IMPLEMENT | Securing the resources, and audit the overall progress and on-going correctness of the aspiration. | Roll out the PLANS and allocate the resources; audit the effectiveness and efficiency of the plans as delivered. | Deploy the resources and audit the effort. GETTING IT DONE! |

The center column, PLANNING, provides ongoing direction as to what's important today and what is coming up on the horizon. The CHOOSING column is about providing vision and guidance. In the absence of an improvement or a change or redirection effort, the leadership process has no meaning or significance, nor is it even needed. Leadership is about moving from *what is* to *what could be*.

One of the more typical causes of negative responses to the question, "Have you experienced any good *leadership* lately?" is that organizations have felt the need for change, but their leaders have failed to get "organized" and make a commitment to it.

## *The Sure Thing*

An audit of Haggle Corp. is presented here. Harry's aspiration was to maintain the status quo, and, in his defense, he truly thought that was good enough, except that he wanted to work a little less. The change he aspired to, presented in the bottom right column, is translated as: "*You* keep on doing what *I've* always been doing." But, without clearly articulating where Harry wanted all this to go (not only to the organization but to himself as well, through completing the work of the CHOOSING column), and without developing the reconciling plan to integrate the choices and the output that O.E. Pickens had generated (through doing the work of the PLANNING column), not much was going to happen, other than exactly what did happen.

**Haggles' LEADERSHIP PROCESS**

|  | CHOOSING | PLANNING | DOING |
|---|---|---|---|
| TARGET | MAINTAIN THE STATUS QUO | If it isn't broke... | If it breaks, call Harry |
| ALIGN | Harry's Historic Behavior | Don't do it unless Harry says | Wait to be told |
| IMPLEMENT | Harry will get it when he's ready | If the wheel isn't squeaking... | Keep on doing what we've always have been doing. |

Harry and Haggle Corp. spent a lot of money and effort, and there was absolutely no positive effect or impact (quite the reverse: it actually hurt the company).

## *The Bottle Rocket*

Another common error is that the top block of the CHOOSING column and nothing else gets done. The new Joe "BA" Hurang over at Higgles Power Zone Inc. had done a great deal to "ring the *bell*" and establish what it was that Higgles had to be and do regarding their customers, among other things. But the *"voice that leads"* was silenced by not carrying out and completing the other seven blocks of work in the *leadership process*.

In effect, he'd **bypassed** all the other blocks and got right into **doing**. The *voice* that leads is loud and prevailing, and "BA's" not completing the work of the leadership process quickly turned into a *story,* translated into "act first, ask questions later." If "BA" had simply gone on to the second block of the Choosing column and defined the Behavioral Principles consistent with his Vision, the disaster with their customers could have probably been avoided. If all nine blocks had been completed, the internal turmoil, false starts, rework, apparent identity crisis, etc. could also have been avoided. It wasn't that "BA" (despite the nickname) was a bad or inept person; he simply had a bad or nonexistent leadership process.

**HIGGLES POWERZONE LEADERSHIP PROCESS**

|  | CHOOSING | PLANNING | DOING |
|---|---|---|---|
| TARGET | "CLOSE TO THE CUSTOMERS" "IMPROVE OURSELVES" | X | X |
| ALIGN | X |  | X |
| IMPLEMENT | X | X | DO IT! |

There are many instances when organizations have experienced a "leadership breakdown." Most breakdowns can be traced back to the omission of at least one or more blocks of the leadership process. Sometimes, an entire column has been leapfrogged in a leader's rush to action. Looking at these columns in the context of vision, strategies, and tactics, the Visionary's work is the Choosing column; the Strategist's work is the Planning column; and the Tactician's work is the Doing column. For success, there has to be Visionary Leadership, Strategic Leadership, and Tactical Leadership. All are necessary.

## *The Journey Continues*

To help understand the model, let's revisit Willie et al. at Willie's Wiggly Lawn Ornaments. When we last left them, they had just finished a very complete and integrated Vision Statement, defined in terms of their four primary stakeholders, around their aspirations for Wiggly. They had stepped up to the "value creation" process for all of the stakeholders, and, in doing so, made the high level strategic choices necessary to allow themselves and the organization to move forward. The Leadership Team (and they had truly become one) had made their choices about how Wiggly needed to transform itself and what it would take to win in the competitive future they "saw." The work of the first block was complete. The output of this work block (The VISION) now became the input for the second block of work, the choices around *aligned behavioral principles*: the new Wiggly CULTURE.

**Culture**, as previously illustrated and defined, refers to an organization's **norm of behavior**. Behavior is about responses to stimuli. A customer call, an interaction with a colleague, a problem, a new piece of information, etc. are all typical stimuli that organizations experience daily. The behavioral response to these stimuli is what defines an organization's culture.

It also sets the standard for "fitting in." People either "fit" or don't "fit," and this is determined based on their behavioral responses. One of the profound personal revelations that Willie and each member of the Wiggly Lawn Ornaments Inc. Leadership Team experienced after they completed the Vision was the feeling that none of them "FIT" in the future they had just defined. Their collective current behaviors were "outliers" or "maverick" in the context of their Vision statement and the new culture the Vision implied.

Sam, Wiggly Lawn Ornaments Inc.'s senior purchaser had passed his recent experience with the Vendor Selection Process Team on to a member of the Leadership Team. He recounted how he'd felt like he'd "landed on another planet." All his instincts, when first exposed to the team's output, were "out of sync." But, he also acknowledged that the team had really done their homework, and had completed a really "nice piece of work." After he had gotten into the content and work of what the team had done around factually documenting the customer cultures of the three *glopata* suppliers, it was a lot easier for Sam to go back to the two disenfranchised suppliers and "lay the cards on the table."

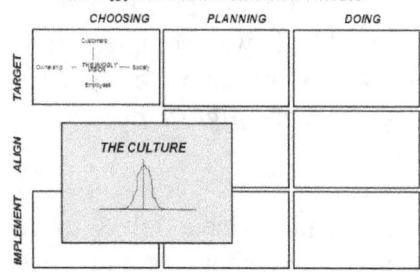

The LT (as the Leadership Team was quickly dubbed) decided to get the Vendor Team in and have them explain how they had gone about auditing a culture and what they had learned (asking subordinates for help was a humbling yet empowering decision for the LT). After only a brief interaction, it became very apparent that this team could really help them. So, Willie et al. disclosed the new Vision. They asked the team to take the Vision and create a set of behaviors that the Vendor Team would expect if they were going into Wiggly Lawn Ornaments Inc. for the first time during their Selection Process.

When the Vendor Team reported back, they confirmed the feelings the Leadership Team had feared to express . . . *they really didn't fit!* They could ring this *Bell* (their Vision), but their *Voice* wasn't ready to be heard (yet). The Vendor Team had been a bit unnerved by Willie and the Leadership Team's request.

In many ways, it was like being asked to tell the "king that he wasn't wearing any clothes." But the Vendor Team, who had begun to see themselves as "mavericks" anyway, decided to go ahead and "let it all hang out." To their surprise, Willie and the LT thanked them profusely. Willie said that he and the Leadership Team were working very hard at the Leadership Process, and the insights of the Vendor Team provided the jump start they needed to get the LT on track and moving through the next block of leadership work. A new *Story* had just been written.

### *"The Truth is Out There!"*

"The truth will set you free," and this was also the case with Willie and the Leadership Team. They had all felt what the Vendor Team was able to express, but denial is sometimes an extremely difficult personal barrier to overcome. The Vendor Team's report was a catharsis. It helped the LT move quickly though the "yeah but" negotiating phase, through depression, and into *acceptance*, and thereby enabled them to get on with their work. They were able to get the "truth" behind them, go out and begin networking, and take a "look-see" at what other organizations and companies had done around *principles*. Some they contacted didn't have a clue as to what was being asked; others had to take a few minutes to dig through their files and "find them," but still others could recite them verbatim, and seemed glad to do it.

When the LT got back together, they had all done their homework, and quickly moved from Individual Awareness to Shared Awareness, from Aims to action (this communication process they adopted was really working). When they were done, they had ten different *Behavioral Principles* that covered the field and, when accompanied by the Vision, they really made sense and gave a feeling of closure and completeness. They felt the "afterglow" again, but this time it didn't last as long because they knew that they had only completed another step and not the journey.

They had chosen an aggressive Vision and cultural shift. At issue now was where they were going to come up with the money, people, time, and organizational effort to make it all happen. This was going to be a lot of work. Work is the expenditure of energy. Where was the "energy" going to come from? Everyone was already "too busy," and budgets, as always, were limited. The Leadership Team was experiencing their first reality check. The rubber was hitting the road, and it was intimidating. Things had been free, easy, and relatively fun up to this point. Expressing your beliefs, philosophies, and principles doesn't "cost" anything; doing something about them does.

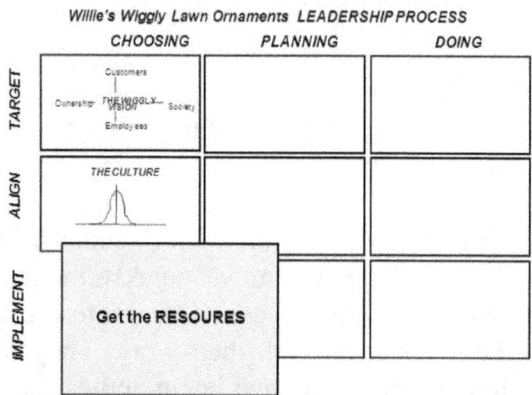

But this was "work" with which the Leadership Team had experience. At least they felt "at home" here. So, they got on with the reality of determining what relevant resources Wiggly Lawn Ornaments Inc. had on hand, and what they didn't have to and would have to get. There was a heap of "didn't-have-to." But, the LT also began to realize that achieving a Vision isn't an overnight thing, and that maybe the Leadership Process was a journey without an end.

Speed was important, but it was just as unrealistic to say, "We don't have the resources to get there this year, so therefore we might as well forget it," as saying, "Let's get it done by January." Care would have to be taken when delivering a timeframe for the Vision. The organization ought to feel "stretched," but they shouldn't feel broken, and they definitely shouldn't feel scuttled. Someone brought up the idea of writing one-year and three-year Mission Statements. But, the consensus was that the LT had done enough "jawing," and needed to get out and do something.

With some regret, yet relief, they cataloged what they had and what resources they felt they could reasonably get, and moved on to the next step of the process: **What & What Order**. "What and What Order" are the high order decisions that have to be made in the face of meeting unlimited demands with limited resources. The Leadership Team was being confronted with having to make some *TOUGH* decisions.

Tough decisions are about having to say NO to other attractive choices by saying YES to the ones you will pursue. All at once, the Team really felt they were getting out of their turf. There was a slow realization that the Team, as it now was composed, didn't have all that was needed to make those tough choices. There were missing pieces of knowledge, information, and expertise that they did not possess.

The Vendor Team had made them realize that maybe they were losing touch with the "ground." They needed help. After some discussion, they decided that they were not the team that should be doing this work. When they got to talking about it, they realized that there were other people in the organization who were in a much better position to do it. With that said, it was time to come out of the closet. Their interaction with the Vendor Team had caused some degree of a stir at Wiggly Lawn Ornaments Inc., and the rumor mill had started, albeit cautiously, to rumble.

The Leadership Team went through a self-audit. Were they ready to come out? The objectives that the Vision had laid out were clear. The difference between who Wiggly Lawn Ornaments Inc. was and who the LT wanted Wiggly to be was easy to sense and feel. Going through the process, particularly the Principles step (the culture shift), had really exposed their own discomforts and resistance to the change, but having gone through it, they felt ready and prepared to talk about it. When one of the team members posed the question, "Are we committed? Are we ready to be the proverbial pig at breakfast?" they all, without hesitation, answered affirmatively. It was time to start involving other people. But how?

### "Out of the Closet"

The LT would really have to do a good job of communicating or this thing could get out of hand quickly. They had gotten word through the Vendor Team about what had happened over at Higgles Power Zone when they had staged their "Revival Rally." They all agreed they sure didn't want any of that. With a flash of insight, a couple of things seemed to come together. The first was that the Communication Process Model the LT had been using worked very well. Why wouldn't it work the same way for the whole organization? The second was that the **motivation** step of the four elements of **leading** involved the transfer of ownership. Wasn't this what the LT was about to undertake? With this revelation, they began the work of planning their "event," the coming out with the new Vision and Principles by which Wiggly Lawn Ornaments Inc. would move forward into the future. But, Willie reflected, "What if someone has new information we didn't consider, or has an insight and Aim different from ours?"

The question was almost rhetorical, for they all realized that the question wasn't really about *if*, it was about *how much* and *how many*. They concluded that this was the way it should be, and the design of the "event" ought to deal with this certainty. After a brief discussion, the "event" that Wiggly's Leadership Team decided to hold was not a one-day HAPPENING, but an ongoing PROCESS.

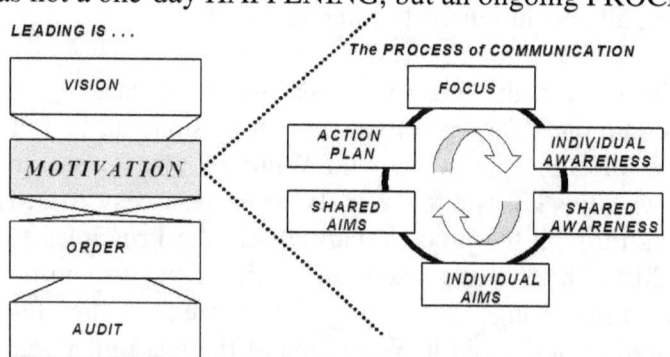

Willie and the Wiggly Leadership Team had come a long way in a relatively short period of time. The fear and intimidation they had all felt when they had gotten into this had vanished. They felt prepared and ready.

With that, they began the task of designing the *process* using the Communications Model, but realistically concentrating on the first two steps, Individual and Shared Awareness, for the initial meetings. When they went out and asked for a "little help" (something they had learned was that if you want help you have to ask for it), they were amazed that the skills to organize and design something like this already existed in the organization. Willie reflected that there was so much potential in the organization just sitting there, ready and waiting for opportunities. The process design came together quickly, and the rollout of the process began. The objective was to engage every member of Wiggly Lawn Ornaments Inc. within two days.

Once the *process* was started, the next thing to amaze Willie and the LT was the amount and quality of the feedback that started rolling in. The LT and the design team hadn't really anticipated anything like this. After a quick huddle of the LT, someone went back into the bag of "charm school stuff" and pulled out a tool called the Affinity Diagram. It said it could organize large amounts of data based on common relationships and similarities. They decided to put it to the test, and again asking for help, put together an ad hoc team to take the feedback and apply the tool. The very next day after the initial process step of Individual Awareness had been completed; the ad hoc team came back with the following.

### **_Elephants, Tigers, and Bears . . . OH MY!_**

The *facts to be considered* listed all supported the changes that the Vision implied. They all supported the need for the Culture shifts the LT had designed. What was shocking was some of the things that were going on. They were worse than anything the LT had discussed, and they all were backed up with facts. Willie was upset, wondering when he had gotten "out of the loop." All this was going on and he hadn't been aware of it. The data was hard. The other two areas of feedback were "soft." The *process* had unearthed the exact fears and concerns that the LT had expressed about themselves (*What will happen to me?* and *Will I be able to do what is needed?*). One thing that was clear was that, before any big thrusts could be launched, the soft people issues would have to be reconciled.

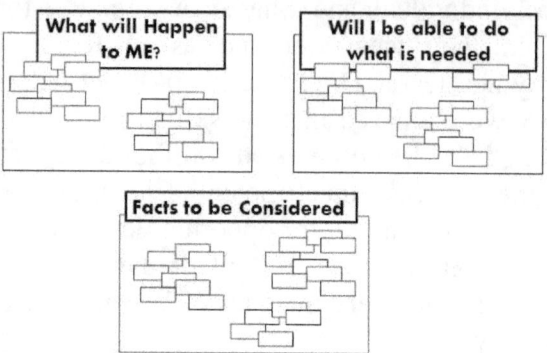

By way of immediate feedback, the Leadership Team communicated back the output of the Affinity Diagram to confirm they had heard. They also communicated that they, the Leadership Team, shared the same concerns, and: A) Everyone would still have a job. Core to the Wiggly Lawn Ornaments Inc. Vision was growth. The job might not be the same as the one they had today, but it would be there; B) Wiggly had a tradition of standing by its people. When new skills were called for, people would be trained and able (and it would start with the Leadership Team). That said, the people of Wiggly weren't exactly put at ease, but they believed in Willie and the team. There had been a lot of openness and disclosure from the Leadership Team during the presentations. And it was all <u>**we**</u> and no <u>**you**</u> when the problems and opportunities were presented. The *bell* that had been rung got the organization's attention. The organization was now waiting for the *voice*.

At the same time, Willie was wondering out loud to the Leadership Team whether they had bitten off more than they could chew or unleashed a "monster." Again, they did a self-audit. They'd expected feedback, maybe not so strong or with as many teeth, but feedback all the same, which would have to be dealt with and integrated. The vision had definitely raised the bar. The feedback confirmed it. If there hadn't been this kind of feedback, they reflected, it would have meant they either didn't do a good job of expressing what it was they wanted for the Wiggly Lawn Ornaments

Inc. organization, or that what they thought was a giant step was, in the organization's eyes, "a walk in the park." They concluded that the "monster" was confirmation they were on the right track. The "rumor mill" was very supportive of what they had presented. The ball was clearly in their court.

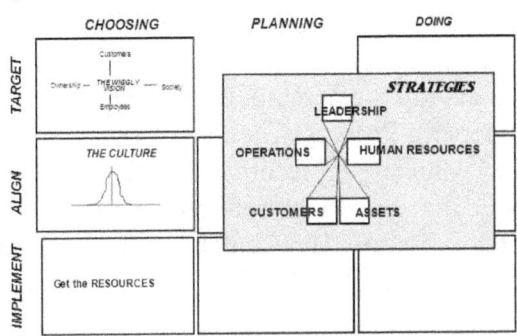

What was also clear from the feedback was that as they went about making the choices of **What** and **What Order**, the Human Resource piece was going to have to lead. The other thing, coming more clearly into focus, was that in many ways they, the Leadership Team, weren't as in touch with reality as they should be in order to go forward with the next step. It was time to get the right knowledge and understandings in place. The Leadership Team wasn't the right mix to do the work. The question the LT was now faced with was, "Who was the right mix?" Should they just expand the size of the LT, or should it be an entirely new team, composed of entirely different people? If it was, how was the LT going to retain "control," or would the LT be seen as abdicators? If they just made the LT bigger, would the LT itself breakdown? Getting to the point where there was real openness, trust, and collaboration had been tough. Would they carry that over with "subordinates" among them? With that, Willie suggested that the LT go back to their Behavioral Principles. The answer to their questions probably ought to come from there.

## *"If you don't do it, someone else will!"*

Arlans General Co. had gone through the same work and agonized over many of the same things Wiggly Lawn Ornaments

Inc. was now struggling with. Arlans had as operating Behavioral Principles strong statements around empowerment, delegation, and process ownership. They had started up as a fairly traditional vertical organization, but had rapidly made the transition to a horizontal (process oriented vs. structurally oriented) company once they had set up and engaged in their Leadership Process.

They had set up ownership for the three distinct activity layers of the Leadership Process. The Choosing Column was owned by the Arlans CEO and the "Executive" staff, plus a facilitator and support personnel. That team was referred to in Arlans as the SLT (Strategic Leadership Team). The Center Column was owned by the PLT (Planning Leadership Team), with only one carryover from the SLT, and mostly consisting of leaders closer to the action. The Doing Column was owned by the TLT (Tactical Leadership Team). Furthermore, each block of work was operated and owned by a separate team (although as yet unlabeled). People at Arlans found themselves dispersed and pulled in by the Leadership Process Blocks on an as-needed basis.

ARLANS LEADERSHIP PROCESS

|  | CHOOSING SLT | PLANNING PLT | DOING TLT |
|---|---|---|---|
| TARGET | Customers, VISION, Ownership, Society, Employees | LEADERSHIP STRATEGIES, OPERATIONS, HUMAN RESOURCES, CUSTOMERS, ASSETS | TACTICS |
| ALIGN | THE CULTURE | The STRATEGIC PLAN | TACTICAL PLANS A–B–C–D–E |
| IMPLEMENT | Get the RESOURCES | Allocate the Resources | GET IT DONE! |

To outsiders, it appeared chaotic and unstructured, but the process provided order, and the speed of progression from decision to action was incredible. The people at Arlans were not only comfortable with this arrangement, but also enthusiastic. When people at Arlans' General were surveyed (part of an ongoing Employee Satisfaction auditing process), it was revealed that, at one time or another, everyone either had been, or expected to be, asked to participate in one or more of the Leadership Process blocks of work. Arlans had gained complete ownership and buy-in to the Leadership Process, and they soon realized that process and the ownership of not only it, but also its outputs, were competitive qualities that few were going to match, particularly at Higgles Power Zone Inc. Inc. and Haggle Corp.

Leadership isn't only people and titles. It's people working in a process. Bad leaders are far and few between. Bad leadership processes are the rule. Good leaders in a bad process are not going to have good outcomes.

# CHAPTER V – To *CHARTER*

"The wise do in the beginning what fools do in the end."

> ***Verbs of Change - CHARTER***
> ***Verb*** to establish, enable, or convey by charter to hire, rent, or lease for usually exclusive use
> ***Noun*** a written document or contract executed in due form

To CHARTER is to "franchise." A Charter grants the right to be and exercise powers. CHARTERING is delegation, the transfer of authority and accountability to those who have the capability and knowledge equal to the task, and who will respond responsibly. Chartering delivers a framework of order within which those being chartered can freely, and with speed, exercise their franchise. Chartering is unleashing the capability and potential that is resident in all organizations.

To get a handle on chartering, there are a few key words that must be understood and differentiated. They are *accountability*, *authority*, *responsibility*, *delegation* and *abdication*. Accountability and Authority are *externally* given. They come from outside an individual or team. *Responsibility* is something that comes from within, a personal feeling or *sense*. Delegation is the *transfer* of ownership; abdication is *renouncing* or effectively "walking away" from ownership. Accountability implies that there will be an answering or accounting for one's *actions* to someone or something else. Responsibility implies the same thing, but also that the person is answerable for a *trust* that was mutually felt and understood.

Authority is about *power*, or, in the context of accountability, the where-with-all to successfully carry out what one is being held accountable for. Revisiting the Success Triangle, Accountability/Authority/Responsibility fit as depicted here. When you think about it, how can a person be held accountable for a poor outcome when that/those person(s) did not have the authority to accomplish an alternate outcome? Conversely, there are instances in which the authority was given, but the accountability wasn't communicated and understood, generating equally poor outcomes. Delegation is the *transfer* of **both** accountability and authority.

Transferring one without the other is abdication. The outcome is certain, and it won't be good. When someone misuses or fails to use the authority and accountability transferred to them, they betray a trust that was present when the accountability and authority were given. They have not acted responsibly.

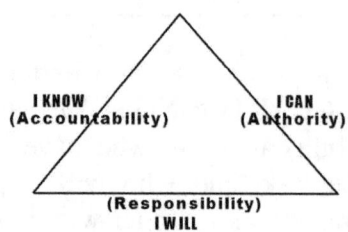

Giving the car keys to a fourteen-year-old who has no experience or driver training and saying, "Make sure you bring the car back in the same condition it left in!" is flat out abdication. Delegation is giving the car keys to an eighteen-year-old (a Driver's Ed course, a license, and three years of operating experience under his/her belt) with the same admonition. If the eighteen-year-old drives recklessly and crashes the car, they had the *Authority* (the Training, Experience, and the keys) and the *Accountability* (a personal reminder that it is not a good thing to ruin the car) to accomplish the desired outcome. What the eighteen-year-old failed to do was act *responsibly* with the car; they violated a trust. The analogy also holds true in organizational settings.

## *Churn Time*

Chartering is the delegation of Authority and Accountability to those who will act responsibly. In any organization, all of the authority and accountability is resident at the top. A CEO, Owner, President, Chief-Cook, etc. have the ultimate accountability for their organization, and the commensurate authority to discharge that accountability. In a traditional vertical organization, the highest-ranking individual doled out authority and accountability to their staff. From there, it trickled down vertically into the organization through staff lines that, in most cases, were functional in nature.

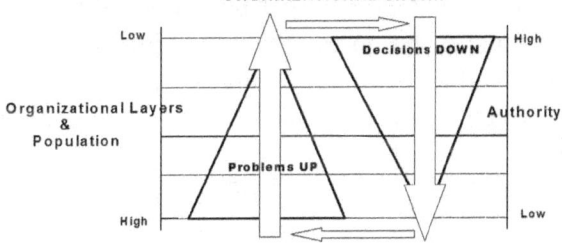

Overlaid on this was a control mentality emanating from the work culture Theories of the period, but dominated by the infamous Theory X, the mother of all excuses and also the mother of *organizational churn*. Churn describes the condition whereby problems that surface on the "shop floor" must "percolate" up to the top for resolution (because "the floor" has neither the accountability nor the authority to deal with them), and direction and solutions then "drip" back down. Smaller organizations, where most things are "in the line of sight," can get away with this kind of control scenario. The scope of endeavor is within a few people's grasp, and these people are relatively accessible, so the resulting churn time is generally short. As organizations grow with success and increase their scope of endeavor, the churn time increases nonlinearly, and, along with it, there is decreasing effectiveness and considerable wasted energy and effort. Such organizations ultimately get bogged down when the "few" approved to deal with all the issues reach their limits. .

Some organizations combated churn time and its inherent lack of speed and agility with downsizing and management layer reductions. The premise was that if you got rid of the "churners," speed and agility would improve. But, the results, in most cases, got worse. The problem was that the *process* didn't change (percolate/trickle). The churn process was still there, but the people who were experts at expediting churn were gone, and the capability of those remaining was exceeded.

### *Chunk & Charter*

A tool that emerged during this time period was *chartering*. One hypothesis of downsizing was that if people were overloaded long enough, they'd figure out how to get unloaded, although in periods of downsizing, that's not something people rush to do. The "downsized" reached out to chartering to off some of the load. Chartering really came into its own when it was combined with the concept of chunking.

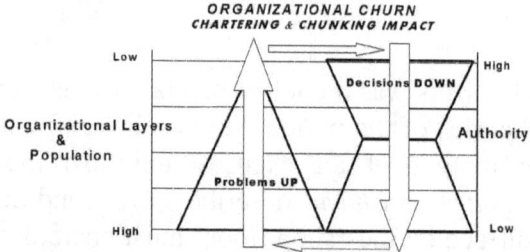

Chunking is taking bite-sized pieces of a problem, solution, or an organization that can be separated and looked at as semiautonomous. With chartering and chunking, Authority and Accountability were moved closer to the action level, and enabled self-direction and self-management to a degree. This move generated the out of phase relationship depicted above (sometimes referred to as "flinching" or "sort-a-kind-a" empowerment).

Only when the barriers of functional stovepipes and power domains were dealt with through moving from a functional vertical structure to a horizontal process and multifunctional process ownership did the shape of the authority and the population density begin to mirror each other. What also materialized was a new level of organizational speed that had never been experienced before. Chartering empowered the organization to deal with its issues when and where they were occurring. Only those issues that were perceived as strategic or impacting "below the water line" were pushed up for resolution and action. Performance on the "shop floor" was owned by the shop floor, and the authority to act was there as well.

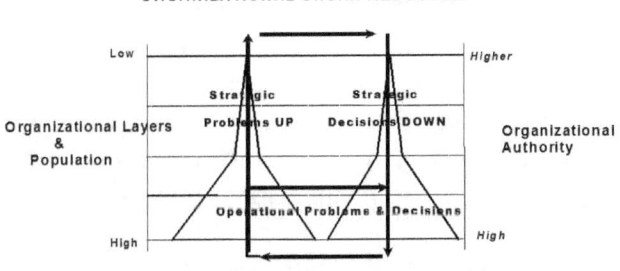

The *"horizontal shunt"* was the product of empowerment through *chartering*. It not only impacted speed, but also the quality and consistency of the "daily" operations of an organization, and thereby an organization's overall performance. The *shunt* also enabled the senior leadership to do the work of senior leadership by taking the burden of resolving daily problems off of them. The "shop floor" was taking care of today's time horizon, while the senior leadership was able to focus on much longer time horizons and competitive positioning.

## 5W2H + 5Q's

Chartering has become a fairly common behavior of leadership. What it accomplishes and what the results are is clear. But, how to charter effectively isn't as clear. A charter ought to answer the basic journalistic questions of who, what, where, when, why, and how (including how much, how many, etc.). The more complete the answer, the better the charter.

Effective answers to those questions come from doing the necessary homework and good preparation. The following is a set of five basic questions that should be part of the preparation prior to chartering, and whose answers ought to be known before embarking. In the context of *chartering*, **"this"** can either be a task with a specific beginning and end, proposals for a work process, an autonomous business, or any "chunk" that makes sense and can be understood by the organization. "This" is the shift, change, or perceived improvement proposed for organizational undertaking.

1. In order to make *"this"* worth doing, what is the **least** we must achieve with respect to making the changes we have visualized, and how will we measure it?
2. What is the **most** or maximum we can hope for *"this"* if we make these changes, and how will we measure it?
3. What **demands** is *"this"* going to place on our resources and on us?
4. In the context of the organization as a whole, what will *"this"* **contribute**?
5. And, how does *"this" **fit*** with the overall plans and aspirations we have for the organization?

Answers to these questions will provide an effective foundation and adequate focus to begin the process of defining the charter.


## *"They what?!?!*

Let's go back and revisit Joe "BA" Hurang at Higgles Power Zone Inc. "BA," despite his good intentions, had gotten a tactic (equipment automation) out in front of a strategy due to the absence of a disciplined leadership process. How this had gone down was pretty typical. The VP of Engineering, John Gear, had gone into "BA's" office with one of Higgles' bright new engineers, and laid out the automation proposal package. "BA" was the "bottom-line" type who immediately flipped through the handout to the back summary page, bypassing 95% of the presentation the new engineer had prepared. Who wouldn't say yes to a "good news" summary page? John (having previous sales experience) knew enough to clam up once the sale was made and "head on down the road." The new engineer, not knowing a whole lot about the ins-and-outs of what went on at Higgles, plunged into the production design and procurement, assuming everything else would take care of itself. "It was in the handout." The first clue manufacturing, HR, or anyone else got about what was going on was when the 18-wheelers pulled up to the warehouse loading docks to deliver the new equipment. With John Gear invoking "BA's" backing, the organization picked up the best they could and ran head on into the solid wall of reality.

Even in the absence of a comprehensive leadership process that would have provided the decisions and alignment around strategies and automation tactics, the disaster could have been avoided if "BA" and his staff had done their homework and gone through the work of ***chartering*** the automation project. The worth of automating, what Higgles could least expect, and the maximum they could hope for was clear. The project's value and overall fit were intuitively obvious in the context of "BA's" Revival Rally and his personal wishes. The demands that moving forward with the automation project would put on the resources of the organization would have been equally clear, had "BA" asked and answered the questions. There was a lot more needed for success than just equipment changes. Without doing the front-end work of organizational alignment and ownership, the backend of an improvement initiative is in the hands of sheer luck. Good chartering requires comprehensive thinking and decisions upfront. In "BA's" case, it seemed like he was running into nothing but bad luck.

### *You Make Your Own Luck!*

Over at Arlans General Company, Higgles Power Zone Inc.' bad luck was quickly parlayed into Arlans's good luck. Every time Higgles Power Zone Inc. staggered, Arlans was ready and waiting to pick up the slack. They had not only installed a leadership process, but they had also converted their whole organization over to a process culture under the leadership of CEO Billy Bob Neighbor. Billy Bob had seen the future before it got there and embraced it. He'd done his research and recognized the cultural vulnerability of Haggle Corp. and Power Zone. He had come on board several years back to "turn Arlans around." To the surprise of many at Arlans, Billy Bob wasn't a cut-and-slash artist. He was an organization and team builder. He'd flattened the organization all right, but he'd also redeployed all the senior experience that was resident in the management's "churn" layers into leading new improvement initiatives. Success was feeding success, and Arlans had such momentum going that if you weren't paying attention (and Haggle and Power Zone weren't) Arlans was becoming awfully hard to catch.

**Arlans Value Adding Process**

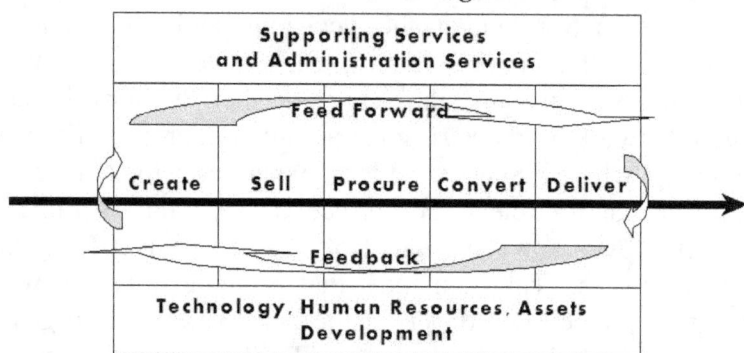

Billy Bob had orchestrated a renewal through the complete transition from functional ownership to business ownership, from the vertical functional stovepipes to cross-functional process ownership teams. There were still functional "heads" with conventional titles, but their charter had been changed from "run your function and meet your functional objectives" to "advance the skills and thereby performance of those functioning in your area of expertise to facilitate, coach, and lead the improvement of Arlans' General." These functional heads also worked with Billy Bob to form the SLT (the owners of the left-hand column of their Leadership Process). The *"create through delivery process"* was now essentially seamless when compared to the "over the wall" and "handoff" mentality that had pervaded Arlans' General's culture before the shift from the vertical culture.

The total Value Adding Process had a Charter, and all of the Work Processes that made up the whole had their individual and aligned Charters. "Show me your Charter!" had started out as a friendly jibe in the beginning, but after a while, it wasn't a joke anymore. The expression became a reminder to everyone about how each was connected and plugged in, and of their significance and value to the organization. In this case, Charters had been used not for a task, but to give ongoing, floor-level direction and meaning to what and why things were happening, and also what was supposed to happen. The Charters also bound everyone together under the same performance parameters, a prerequisite for teaming.

## *The Paradox of Power*

Billy Bob had met and faced the paradox of power that states that to get power you must give it away. He realized that a leader wasn't going to be very powerful if that leader was heading up a gaggle of powerless individuals. Conversely, the more powerful those that he aspired to lead became, the more powerful he would become. At issue was how do you "give" power away? The solution was the act of chartering. Arlans' General discovered that the Charters provided an order that had never been experienced before. There was an openness that allowed understanding that, in turn, advanced a feeling of caring throughout Arlans' General. As "mushy" as it seemed, people were eager, although at first hesitant to admit it, to get to work. It was rapidly becoming a fun place to be. The "killer" stress of internal friction and adversarial relationships was gone. The stress of hard work never killed anyone, and, in fact, it's therapeutic. Billy Bob was also vigilant in keeping the Charters up with the capabilities of the people in the process. As the skills and capabilities increased, so did the authority and accountability. In the beginning, it was all Billy Bob pushing. At some point, it had flipped the other way around, and the organization was pulling to change the boundaries.

A Charter establishes the "field of Play," the fence lines and boundaries, the resources available, the authority and accountability, and the expectations and measures of success. It states: "This is what you own. This is what you have accountability and authority over. This is what's expected." It opens up lines for dialogue and feedback, as well as feed-forward. It provides a framework of objective measurement for ongoing progress and verification of expectations. It eliminates the "hurry up and wait" syndrome, a chronic predicament of leadership who have not cleared the way by making the upfront decisions that are needed.

## *The Learning Zone*

Another powerful application for chartering is when organizations venture into the *learning zone*. The Learning Zone is an area outside of the existing culture that does not reflect current "behavior," but is believed to be of value and something the organization should move towards. It might be an internal feature, such as the initial move from vertical to horizontal; or an external move, like a venture into a supplier alliance or a more connected customer relationship. Chartering is an effective and orderly way of piloting a change, learning from it, and, if successful, developing the basic data and expertise to deploy it broadly.

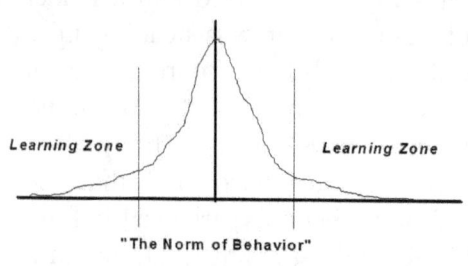

Back at Wiggly Lawn Ornaments Inc., Willie and the new SLT (the old LT) were being inundated with ideas and changes coming back through the Leadership Process. Among the many were requests to move forward with "empowered teams" and "cellular" ideas.

Some days, Willie et al. felt as though they had unleashed a juggernaut. Their Leadership Process was continually challenging them to change their ideas and old patterns of behavior. But, they discovered "relief" could always be found in the Choosing Column work that they had completed, particularly in the Behavioral Principles block of work.

Wiggly Lawn Ornaments Inc. had been set up and run like a lot of companies. They had divided up the "work" into the smallest possible bits and pieces, and had made people accountable for their incredibly small piece only, with no connection to any others. This extended from the shop floor up through "mahogany row."

Expanding accountability and authority was a bit uncomfortable for the SLT, and it was especially uncomfortable and threatening to the cadre of first-line supervisors that the Wiggly Lawn Ornaments Inc. current operating culture depended on (the *boss*). The proposals fit the Wiggly vision and principles, and it looked like a single solution to a bundle of problems. What the SLT decided to do was have the PLT take it on, carve out a section of Wiggly where the support and ownership for the idea was the highest, and have them write a Charter to launch the initiative. The SLT had been pondering taking on the vertical/horizontal culture issue across the board, but had always pulled back, recognizing they just didn't have the knowledge, expertise, or resources.

Going ahead with a smaller unit was within the Wiggly Lawn Ornament's "headlights," and it would give them the field-testing they really needed if this was going to be deployed throughout Wiggly. It also allowed the majority of the first-line supervision to watch, learn, and get a concrete sense of "where this was all going." Using *chartering* in this context, venturing into the learning zone, is a way of providing order for not only the smaller team that was chartered to make the change, but also for Wiggly Lawn Ornaments Inc. as a whole. The rest of Wiggly would have the benefit of the experience, but more importantly, start building ownership in a way that would ensure "their necks weren't on the line."

## *The Dark Side*

Chartering is always an issue of "too" . . . too tight, too loose, too bold, too milk toast, too everything. But, of particular issue is a Charter that is written to manipulate. Manipulation is a hangover from a control culture. It goes beyond too tight to this is the only possible outcome.

The sinister definition of manipulate is to change by artful or unfair means, especially to serve one's own purposes. Manipulation is so transparent in today's organizations that you'd think it would be a footnote in a textbook. But, it is still practiced. The root cause is usually a lack of *leadership's personal alignment* around "bells" that have been rung, particularly "empowerment." Many leaders get into empowerment way before they themselves are ready or have a clear idea what they are going to empower an organization with or for. Without this preparedness or a leadership process that defines where the authority and accountability for a range of decisions are going to reside, it's impossible to empower.

A darker use of Chartering is in those instances when a leader isn't ready to let go, yet wants to appear that he is letting go, or worse, "let's go" in an instance when he should clearly be the one making the decisions. Either way, it always results in an outcome that "poisons the water" for a long time to come, and becomes fodder for pinning another cartoon strip up on the bulletin board.

Back at Haggle Corp., Harry Huckster was still smarting from the mess that "O.E. Pickens had left behind." People had stopped coming to his open door Thursday meetings, and he had picked up the sarcastic "visit to the King" comment through the grapevine. The only good news, as Harry saw it, was that people still knew who was "in charge around here."

But, Harry's workload was still there. Nothing had changed, including Harry's desire to lighten his load. At a neighborhood cocktail party one Friday night, Harry got entranced by a neighbor talking about all the good things his company was able to do with "Chartering." Harry pursued it further on Saturday, and got all the "go-by" material and information "on this chartering thing." By late Saturday night, Harry had craftily shaped a Charter that would get what "he wanted."

On Monday morning, Harry called in the anointed (who numbered two) and delivered the "Charter." There was a stunned silence after the two had read through the Charter. Harry interpreted that as positive feedback. The "fence line" Harry had crafted into the Charter was so tight that there were no decisions to make. Unknowingly, Harry had just expanded the *stories* that guided Haggle Corp. Specifically, Harry "was the man," but even more dubious, "Harry was slipping." If Harry had picked up his files, gone down the hall, dumped them on someone's desk, and said, "Do it!" people would have understood. But this Charter left people wondering, "What the heck was this all about?" Harry was quickly losing the confidence of those whom he needed the most.

## *Feeling the FORCE*

Chartering, without a doubt, is a tool and a leadership behavior that will produce results, one way or the other. Accountability and Authority are powers that can produce a lot of good when put in the hands of those who will act responsibly. Another way of thinking about this (from a control side) is that chartering is "bestowing a work permit." Leadership owns the ultimate NO in any organization. The people of an organization own the ultimate YES. Chartering is an effective, orderly way to construct the NO circle, and expand the possibilities of what people can say YES to. It is a way that really gets into the potential to advance that organization's purposes that is resident in organizations. There is a force in every organization that, until tapped, will never be felt. The leadership behavior of Chartering is the tap.

# CHAPTER VI – To *CHART*

"If you don't know where you are . . . you're lost."

> ***The verbs of Change - CHART***
> **Verb** to make a map or chart of
> **Noun** an outline, map, exhibiting something (climatic or magnetic variations) in its geographical context

CHARTING is a catalyst of creativity. This activity more than others causes fundamental perception shifts which, in turn, unleash innovation, the fuel of improvement. It is as true today as it was centuries ago for the great explorers. CHARTING or MAPPING removes the cloak of "subjectivity" and replaces it with "objectivity." Seeing what and how things truly get done and how decisions are made is power.

Charting your ***work processes*** for the first time in the context of your organization's purpose is an awakening. However, once you get through the denial and anger phase, and move into acceptance, things get better -- ***quickly***. "Chart, map . . . who needs it! I know what's going on around here and what's broke and needs fixing. What a waste of time!" The usual "what's broke" the speaker has in mind is some poor, unsuspecting "culprit" struggling along, doing the best anyone can with a faulty work process. Work process charting or mapping is the only effective way to uncover the "truth that is out there." It is a vehicle to see *cause*. Without establishing cause, it is sheer luck if any solution acted on will work. More probable is that, just to stop the "beatings," the problem gets pushed upstream or downstream by the "culprit," who receives the "beatings" from the person who knows ". . . what's broke and needs fixing."

A *process* is defined as a series of actions or operations conducing to an end. A huge mental barrier to breakthrough is seeing process in everything an organization does. It's easily seen in manufacturing, where the array of equipment performing value-adding steps comes together to produce a finished product. It's easy to see in any repetitive type work, from complaint handling to invoicing. Where it gets more difficult to see is in areas of work that are on much longer repetitive cycles, or where one person has been doing all the work. But, if one looks, they will find it.

## "We want to be just like whom?"

In manufacturing, one of the highest order documents is what's usually referred to as a *Process Flow Sheet*. It describes how raw materials flow into the operation, and the actions and transforms that take place, up to and including the final step of releasing the finished good. Another profound understanding in manufacturing is that a process can't be improved until it is *standardized*. Until it is, there is nothing to compare it to in terms of better or worse. Outside of manufacturing, one of the most easily seen examples of process and standardizing is in the fast food service sector, or anything involving franchising. Franchising is the zenith of work process mapping and standardization, which most everyone has contact with continually. There is a wealth of understanding and insight that can be gained by getting "out of the box" and comparing your work or business to *"Mickey D's."*

Charting is visual. There are many different protocols for the use of symbols and associated activities. The symbols from the electronics field are similar but different from those used, for example, in the chemical processing industry. The important thing, in any case, is to decide upfront on a list of symbols and their uses. In some cases, rivers, trees, rapids, mountains, etc. have been used as symbols to overcome common language barriers in multinational situations. These are the basic symbols and their meanings.

## *"Queue Time"*

When Arlans' General started their transition from a vertical structure mindset to a horizontal process driven organization, they had worked on their Leadership Processes first. What they discovered through charting was the huge amount of time consumed by "queue time" or DELAY. The implementation of the changes wasn't going well not because they were making the wrong choices or had "bad" people, but because the existing process was layered with approvals and people essentially "checking the checkers." When they initially charted the work process, a procedural change went through for approval and implementation. They asked the clerk who initiated the change to attach to the proposal a log sheet requesting each person to note the day and time that they had "signed off" and passed it on to the next recipient. The procedural change ultimately required staff level approval. Some of the doubters on the SLT felt pretty smug, and firmly believed that things were a whole lot better than the newcomer Billy Bob Neighbor hypothesized they might be. In "fun," they set up a pool around the day and time the proposal would reach staff for approval.

After the first week went by and the proposal hadn't shown up, 30% of the SLT were already out of the running. After three weeks had gone by without anyone seeing it, only Billy Bob and one other were still in the running. At the end of the second month, Billy Bob had won the pool. The SLT was agitated, and wanted to get out and find the "stupid thing." But, Billy Bob prevailed and held the line. In the 16th week, the proposal finally hit the VP of Operations' desk. It was turned around that day, and returned to the clerk who had initiated it for implementation. Two weeks later, it was fully implemented and a "done deal." An 18-week cycle time became the approval and implementation process's baseline performance. During the 16 weeks leading up to approval, the proposal spent all except one day sitting in someone's mailbox, waiting to be acted on. It probably would have been longer had the SLT not been diligently checking every mail delivery. The "approval process" was the routing slip that was attached. When they went back to the clerk and asked about the number currently in the system, they discovered that it was approaching 100. Some had been in the system for over a year. Billy Bob categorized the steps and the times for each and presented the following to the SLT about the "experiment" they had just run.

The whole SLT was dazed by the factual documentation of what it really took to get something "through the system." This had been a simple "no-brainer" procedural change that no one disagreed with. They all wondered out loud how long a controversial one would take, or whether it would ever surface or just be "queued to death."

| STEP | TIME |
|---|---|
| | Preparation and initial transmittal – 1 hr. |
| | Read and Approve (6 people) – ca. 7 hours |
| | "Queue time" between approvals – ca. **16 weeks** |
| | Roll out, training and communication – 2 weeks |
| | Total Elapsed TIME – 18 weeks |

They all agreed the latter was probably the case. The clerk's "outstanding warrants" log was proof of it, and no one offered any sidebar bets. "Queuing" appeared to be the norm of management behavior (one that they all were party to as well) and something they (the SLT) needed to deal with. They had all been advocating that the organization embrace the attribute of speed, but, at the same time, the work process they were all a part of was an embarrassment with respect to speed. This was the SLT's first confrontation with a leadership alignment check.

Arlans' General would experience many "turning points" over the next several months, and this experience provided a big one. The SLT, after their initial disappointment, really hunkered down and looked at the entire Leadership Process, beginning with why this proposal was subject to staff approval in the first place, where it fit in the Leadership Process, and who ought to have the authority and accountability to decide. A year later, they would look back on this event as the defining moment that started the Arlans' General Renewal.

## *The HIDDEN Organization*

When Arlans first got into Work Process Charting with the SLT leading the way with the Leadership process, there had been a lot of cheering and good humor that could be summarized in a word – *finally*! The impact and changes began to be felt immediately. People who had always complained about the sluggishness of management were now on the hot seat themselves in the decision making process. But it was something that everyone had generally wanted and, they were fairly well-prepared for it.

When the practice of charting and process ownership started cascading into the bailiwicks of the day-to-day *"create - sell - buy - make - deliver"* Value Chain, the joking toned down immediately. People had seen what had happened to the management ranks and the "excesses" that had come out of there. Now they were in the "hot seat."

But Billy Bob stayed the course. He said, ". . . nobody is going out. The reward for simplifying and streamlining your work processes isn't going to be no job. We're a growth company, and we need experienced people." It wasn't all the reassurance the organization needed, but it was enough to get them going. Billy Bob had quickly earned the reputation of being a person who says what he means, and means what he says. He was a person whose *bells*, *voice*, and *stories* were well-aligned and tracking over the same ground.

One of the first work processes to be tackled was order entry and scheduling. It was a fairly simple piece, not that complex, and something that customers seemed to be complaining about. The SLT chartered a process ownership team, and gave them their expectations around cycle time improvement and complaint reduction.

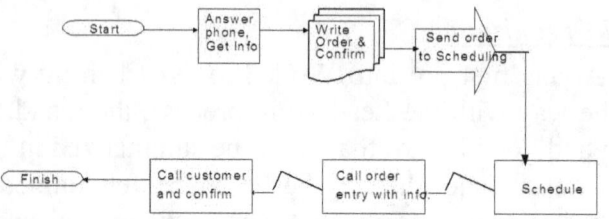

The team had their startup problems with "Who's in charge and what are we supposed to do?" But, they soon got over it, and reached the conclusion that the "who" was "we" and the "what" was in the Charter. For the team, it was the first time they had all ever been in the same room together, and for several the first time they had ever met face-to-face (particularly scheduling and the order entry people). They started with charting the basic process. The result is shown above. After pondering it a bit, the team decided to go out and begin measuring "their" cycle time.

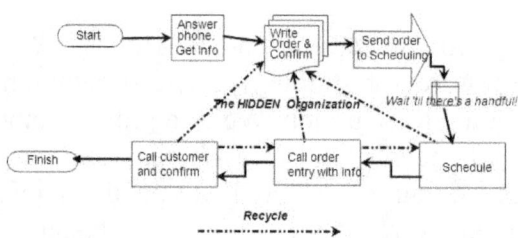

When they got back together in a week, they were all a bit glum. Their simple process was ballooning into a monster. In the preceding week, they discovered that not one order had gone straight through the system. There were *recycle* paths all over the place. Not only that, there was an average elapsed time of well over 48 hours from the initial customer contact to getting back with the first promising ship date, and what's more, the customer never accepted the first ship date, and the process started all over again. They also discovered a lot of "queue time." The people in scheduling weren't there to work with the order, or vice versa, when scheduling called order entry back. They also found orders were only delivered to scheduling "1$^{st}$ thing in the morning" and "right after lunch" because "there usually weren't enough orders there to make it worth the walk." They began charting their new **"Hidden"** Work Process by developing all the recycle lines. By the next meeting, they had collected hard data that said 70% of people's time in "order entry and scheduling" was spent in the *recycle loop*. Not only were they dumbfounded, but so was the SLT when they had their first feedback session at the end of the month. While humbling, it was encouraging. The recycle loop had been a huge source of stress and irritation, not to mention out of sight name-calling. The team set off with a clear mission – crush the *recycle loop* and eliminate queue time. This was "doable" and something the team now **owned**.

## *Success Feeds Success*

When we last left Wiggly Lawn Ornaments Inc., they had just ventured into the "Learning Zone," writing a Charter to explore the horizontally-empowered work environment. The PLT had "chunked and chartered" a piece of Wiggly that was seen as autonomous. So it wasn't seen as posing any big threat to anyone. Besides being seen as autonomous, it was physically isolated off in its own building on one of the manufacturing sites. But what went on there was fairly representative of shop floor operations at Wiggly. The venture had been a huge success.

The project team had come back with productivity figures that showed that 32% of the people's time was spent waiting "to be told." If the supervisors were off at lunch or tied up in a meeting, the operation essentially went down. In other instances, the supervisor wasn't vested with the authority to act, and the supervisor, along with the operating crew, sat and waited for someone "to get back with them." With all the documentation and careful analysis that the project team had developed, the only thing blocking progress was the scary personal stuff of moving forward.

Even though the project team had engaged everyone with what was going on, the proposal for increasing authority and accountability was intimidating. No matter how much everyone grumbles about a lack of authority, in comparison, life is pretty easy when your only accountability is to show up for work on time, do what you are told, and don't leave before quitting time. But, the project had been a small enough chunk of the organization that there was enough outside support to do a thorough job of training and provide the needed support and coaching to move the new process owners on their way to success.

What Wiggly Lawn Ornaments Inc. had accomplished was a real life working model for success that the whole organization could have contact with and "feel" not only the change, but also the "need for change" in their personal work processes.

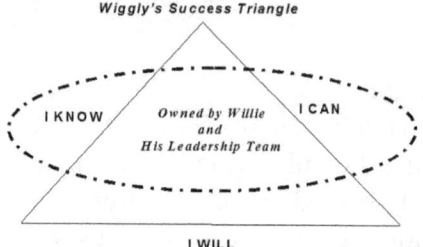

The success had set off a new round of requests up through the Leadership Process. Willie and the "SLT" had quickly come to realize they *owned* the "I Know & I Can" legs of the Success Triangle. The "I Will" leg was turning more into "Why won't you LET ME!" The pressure was really building to get on with it. Willie and the SLT decided they could extend the range of the organization's headlights by redeploying the resources being freed up by the first team's work as coaches and facilitators for the teams that followed. Chartering was taking care of the *I Know*, and these freed up resources would expand the range of *I Can*. Willie and the SLT were discovering that the more successful they became, the more able to be successful they could be. They also began to ponder what they were going to do with the windfall of resources that seemed to be coming out of this. When they had created their Vision and Principles, Human Resources had been one of the biggest restraints in getting on with it. It was time to accelerate the Wiggly Lawn Ornaments Inc. Strategic Plan.

## *"Off with their heads!"*

Over at Haggle Corp., CEO Harry Huckster was in a huff. Business was getting more than soft. Arlans' General was eating their lunch. Not only that, his "open door Thursday meetings" had turned into an embarrassment. People had, for the most part, stopped coming, so when one Thursday a group of people showed up with a proposal, Harry was uplifted, at first anyway.

This group had charted out Haggle's order entry and promising process. They said that customers were really getting agitated with Haggle's response time, and they were beating "us over the head with Arlans' General performance." Harry was "all ears." The team that came in was without a doubt courageous, but they were also considerate. What they brought back to Harry was the "carrot" that they could cut response time by 90% if they could eliminate "queue time" in the order entry and promising work process. "This was more like it," Harry thought to himself.

Harry hadn't heard the first shoe fall, but he really felt the second after he asked the question, "What do we need to do to get rid of this *queue time* thing?" When they answered that over half of it was spent waiting for Harry to get back with pricing approval, Harry's first instinct was to "reach out and touch someone." But, with all the lawsuits and litigation in the newspapers, Harry was able to control himself.

The team would later tell the story of how they weren't sure at that moment whether Harry's head was going to blow clean off, or whether they had just lost their heads. To Harry, the authority to set pricing had always been under his hat, and he prided himself on doing it well. But, as Harry simmered down, he realized the facts that these people had presented with their charting of the work process were irrefutable. There weren't really any more questions to ask. Harry was a stickler for detail, and they had it all. How could he say no?

There was a long silence in the room. There was fear on both sides (Harry that he was losing control and the team fearing they'd just lost their jobs). Harry broke the silence by saying they had done a great job. Their data and facts were complete and compelling. In the history of Harry's Thursday Meetings, this would be the first time Harry didn't come back with a *"**But** . . ."* Instead, Harry said, quietly at first, "Let's do it." There was another long, silent pause. Even Harry couldn't believe what he just said, but it was beginning to feel good. So he said it again, this time with emphasis. A new *story* had just come into being.

## The Truth only hurts when it's True

Over at Higgles Power Zone Inc., old "BA" was continuing to fall all over himself. His Revival Rally had set things into motion and created a level of chaos that Higgles had never experienced before. "BA" wondered, "How could something that felt so good in the beginning turn into such a nightmare."

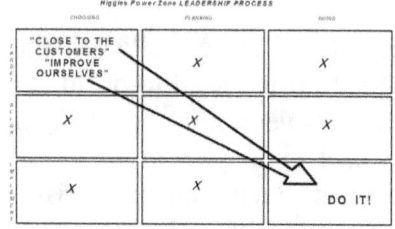

Jim Spin (VP HR) came in with the answer. He'd followed up with his contacts after the Revival Rally's impact had started to be felt and discovered that the Rally was not the end; it was a beginning. He charted the Leadership Process that he saw, and pointed out to Harry all the missing pieces of work. It was humbling for Jim to do it.

Seeing what really happened and how he'd been a part of it hurt. El ("BA's secretary) walked in at that moment, and "BA" gave her a summary and asked for an opinion. El was among the first to get "burned" after the Rally, so there was a bit of hesitation, but then it all came out. "Bottom line," El said, "if you're going to start something like you did, you'd better be prepared to do what it takes to get it done, including cleaning up your own act!" El went on to relate how personally compromised she was by the customer visit incident. Every mountain has a valley, and "BA" and Jim had just fallen to the bottom of it.

## "Let's Get Together"

Work Process *charting* and Mapping isn't just germane to the leadership process. When the first empowered team over at Wiggly

Lawn Ornaments Inc. got through their transition, they really went into high gear. They started charting everything. One of the discoveries they made was how convoluted receiving and releasing raw materials into production was.

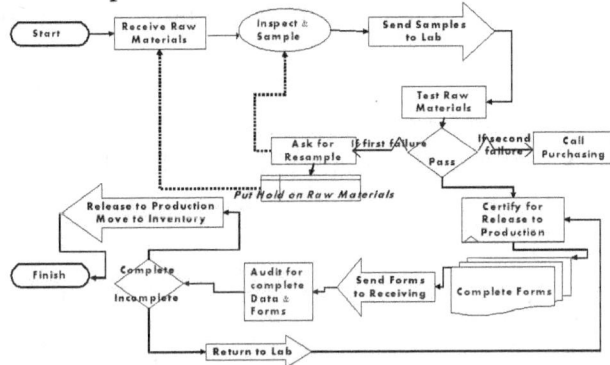

When they got it on paper, somebody said, "If every time I bought something at home, I'd have to go through what I do here, I'd never make it to work." This led to the next thought: "WHY ARE WE DOING THIS???" They called up Sam in purchasing and asked him to stop by. Sam's feathers were still singed from the whole *glopata* affair. He was feeling sort of unloved and unwanted (for a purchasing type unloved was SOP, but unwanted . . .). When Sam got out there, the team confronted him with the problem. They said, "Why are we doing all this testing, clogging up our storage areas and warehouse, when the vendor should have done this already. We should be able to take their stuff right off the truck and roll it into production?" The only answer Sam could think of was, "That's the way we've always done it – and engineering says to do it." After some jawboning, Sam agreed to pick up the ball on this.

Sam's first stop was to see the leader of the Vendor Selection Process Team. Sam recapped the problem and ventured the solution: "Why don't we make the vendor accountable?" After some head scratching, the leader pulled out the files. They discovered that some vendors (Arlans' General was one of them) were already sending their lab data and some were sending the SPC records for the lots the shipments came from. When they checked further, these vendors had not had one shipment rejected or even rechecked in the past 18 months (which was how long the records the team had collected went back). So, the answer to the initial question was obvious. Now, the new question was how to make it happen. Like a light coming on, Sam saw the future. Sam had been a world-class "price hammer." What Sam now needed to become was a world-class "value hammer." "This culture thing," he thought, "was beginning to make a whole lot more sense with everything else going on around here!" Sam embarked on his newly-found mission. In short order, the new "Supplier Improvement Process Team" was chartered, with Sam right in the middle of it. The "Selection Team" was integrated in and it was time to "rock-and-roll."

## *Feeling the Force*

Work Process Charting causes many truths that have been dormant in organizations for long periods of time to surface. It takes a whole lot of organizational courage to get them to surface, and it takes an equal amount of humility to deal with them. It is rare to find an organization that *overestimates* the truths and problems that this activity alone uncovers.

Charting is a powerful leadership behavior. It demonstrates simultaneously both courage and humility. It brings about many opportunities for leaders to make their voices heard. Any leader who rings the bells of cycle times and speed better be prepared with the strong voice of *charting*. Stories will come into being one way or the other if the bell has been rung. Charting isn't just a tool; it's a leadership behavioral way of life.

# CHAPTER VII – To *CHALLENGE*

"Until Challenged, You'll Never Know."

> ***The verbs of Change - CHALLENGE***
> ***Verb***    to dispute especially as being unjust, invalid, or outmoded; to order to halt and prove identity
> ***Noun***    a summons that is often threatening, provocative, stimulating, or inciting; a calling to account or into question

To CHALLENGE is instructive. It is not necessarily noxious, as the word often connotes. Challenging puts "what is" into the context of at least "what should be," and, if you can shed your mental shackles and get out of the box, "what could be." Constructive challenging requires *courage* and energy, but it demands *consideration*. Lacking consideration for people while energetically challenging them is very destructive. Without consideration, calling to question the validity of what a person does challenges the value and validity of the person – it's a *personal attack*.

A competitor who challenges you is your teacher. Being proactive and accountable for your own learning and becoming your own challenger and teacher is making a commitment to strive to be the best. Challenges from competitors, customers, or operating environments continually impact organizations requiring analysis and response. Getting ahead of the wave and not waiting for a competitive test to expose a weakness can result in significant rewards. Knowing an organization's weaknesses and strengths before they are tested by competition, and being able to orchestrate changes to them in the absence of duress, is a competitive advantage.

The various processes leading to creative and innovative solutions to stubborn problems have been studied in some detail. A common attribute is a perception shift, seeing the same old thing from a whole different angle, often through analogy. *Customer Focus*, or seeing your organization through the eyes of your customers, was a perception shift that enabled the industrial leadership breakaways of the '60's and '70's. The perception shift is a non-threatening, *constructive challenging* technique that can facilitate unifying movement away from defending "sacred turf." It manages a self-audit through an entirely different set of lenses. The insights gained can, in turn, enable breakthrough thinking and innovation.

Dueling from well "dug in" positions, typically experienced in adversarial settings, is not constructive challenging. **Constructive challenging** requires **collaborative** thinking and acting, and *ally* or *advocate-like* behavior when someone advances a position of *"why"* or *"why not!" Collaborative challenging* confronts ideas and situations, not people or organizations. It is not win/lose, and it is not win/win. These are both *you/me* situations. *Collaborative challenging* is moving beyond you and me, to *us* and *we*.

Great examples of collaborative challenging are more common in the home than the workplace. Organizational collaboration isn't something that is systematically taught in academia, and challenging in organizational venues is most often thought of in terms of rude or arrogant behavior. *Collaboration* in educational systems is another word for *cheating* or *plagiarism*. *Challenging* in a social setting is synonymous with *provocation*. In terms of cumulative experience with either, most people are still at a low point on the learning curve. There aren't many reward and recognition systems that recognize and elevate collaboration or challenging. Most systems are set up based on individual results, not collaborative results, and "spun" based on behavior. A person who *challenges* is more often thought of as "not a team player" than as an *asset*. Yet, collaboration and challenging are essential attributes of high performance teams, as well as high performance leaders.

### *"You are not being purposeful!"*

Back at Wiggly Lawn Ornaments Inc., Sam, the senior-purchasing guru, had experienced a really bad case of crushed ego. The Supplier Selection Team had trampled all over the old domain of purchasing. After the experience, Sam felt that the 27 years he had spent in the "procurement game" were all for naught. Sam was at a loss as to how to posture both inside and outside of the company. Who was "Sam"? Sam didn't even know for a while. A phone call or interaction always felt like another attack. Sam swung entirely onto the defensive, and, in the words of Sam's spouse, "Into survival mode."

Selling the Supplier Improvement Process Team had gotten Sam out of the funk. But, it only took the first meeting to get back into it. Half the people on the team had been a part of the Vendor Selection Team. They behaved differently and Sam, being somewhat paranoiac by this time, went instantly on the defensive any time a question was asked about ". . . how it had been done."

The initial meeting had not gone well at all. Afterward, Mel (a long time associate and family friend) approached Sam and said, "You need some advice! So clam up and listen!" Mel said that there were three ways to go through life: as a victim, a victimizer, or a servant. "You acted like the first two in that meeting, and that behavior is getting us nowhere!" Mel sketched out what appears here and said, "Call me when you've figured it out." Sam took it home that night and, after *spousal review*, got feedback that even Sam could understand. "Mel called you a reactive, self-centered butt hole." With one barrel emptied, Sam went for broke and asked, "If that's what I am, what did Mel say I wasn't but should be?" The Double "O" answer came quickly. "You are not being purposeful. You aren't serving the team's purposes; you're trying to get the team to serve your purpose." With that, the TV went on. Spouses know a major league sulk coming on when they see one.

The next day, Sam went back to work, and called Mel and disclosed the past evening's epiphany. After a short conversation, Mel said, "I knew you'd figure it out," to which Sam queried, "Now what?" Mel explained the 48-hour rule, and said, "The rest is up to you." Sam quickly got on the horn and called each of the team members. They reluctantly agreed to a short meeting at the end of the day. Sam did a little more thinking and brought the above into the meeting.

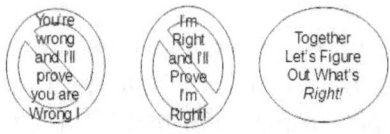

After confessing to acting like a "butt cheek," and thanking Mel for pointing it out, Sam stated that a genuine effort would be put forth to "sin no more." Sam also said that maybe this purposeful behavior was the way to be when approaching suppliers. "Purposeful also means resolved and determined," Sam reflected. "Maybe we, together with willing suppliers, ought to become one *purposeful*, world-class value hammer together." The team was back on its feet. Sam had received an important lesson. The personal behavior of those seen by the organization as its leaders has a huge impact on how an organization will move forward when they are called to challenge the status quo.

## *Defining the Problem*

If anyone sat down and reflected about those occasions when they felt that their ancestry was being brought into question, most would respond that it had been during instances when they were forwarding a "solution." Solutions might range from picking a place to go out to eat, to launching a new product line. Most organizations find themselves embroiled in less-than-collaborative, challenging situations when they are deliberating solutions. Some organizations have gone to the extent of proclaiming they are in the "solution business," a big perception shift in the right direction. Solutions are definitely where the money is, so why all the adversarial, combative challenging?

People spend a good chunk of their time crafting solutions and going on the trail to sell them. They have a very high degree of ownership in what they propose. So, some of it has to do with win/lose and the way individual "batting averages" are kept to decide who gets compensation and recognition. But, the bulk of it comes from the fact that very little time is spent in organizations clearly *defining the problem* in comparison to the time spent arguing about and struggling through solutions that aren't jointly owned.

When the problem is clear and understood, organizations pull together quickly and are able to collaboratively challenge themselves and converge on a solution with relative ease. Those instances in which organizations experience "emergencies" and there is a "clear and present" sense of what has "happened" are instances in which collaboration and collaborative challenging surface quickly. After the "emergency" is gone, people will reflect back on their experience as one of the most satisfying in their career.

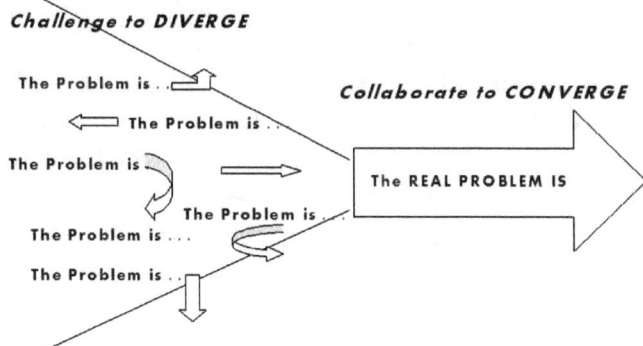

The simple fact is that reasonable people, when confronted with the same information, will generally arrive at shared conclusions. The root cause of stumbling in the solution phase in non-emergency situations is that people aren't seeing and owning the same problem to solve. Great solutions start with great problem definition. Collaborative challenging in problem definition will minimize the tendency of non-collaborative challenging and inefficiency in the solution phase.

## "Mirror, Mirror, on the wall . . .

Back at Harry's Haggle Corp., Harry Huckster's "unleashing" authority and accountability for pricing decisions had opened the door again to the alternate Thursday "ritual." People still saw it as a risk to go in there, but the pricing decision had demonstrated there was an "upside." One Thursday a group had called ahead, asking for a 3-hour block of time. It was unusual to ask for that much time, but Harry agreed. The pricing thing had really gone well, and had freed up a significant amount of Harry's time. He was really looking for the next opportunity.

The group arrived and asked Harry to participate in a process *with them*. They brought the Communications model. This put Harry in a different role than his usual judge and jury standing, but Harry agreed without comment. The group said that together they wanted to work through and reach a shared awareness of what the *problem* was with Haggle's current market position in the context of its competitors, customers, and market environments. They suggested and got Harry's agreement that the best way to do this was to converge on a *problem statement* split into two pieces. The first piece was exclusively reserved for FACTS. They called it "*The Situation.*" The second piece was reserved for *hazy* facts, PERCEPTIONS, and editorial opinions. They called that "*Consequences*."

The group came with a ton of facts and a balanced number of opinions. Harry rose to the occasion with a set of his own. During the Individual Awareness phase, everyone had an equal right to be heard and express what he or she knew, along with their understanding of what it meant. Harry warmed up to the process quickly (to the surprise of all, including Harry). After the appointed three hours were up, Harry was the first to say, "Let's keep on going." At about 7:30 that evening, the meeting broke up. Harry had called in extra people who were better able to fill some of the voids, and they had quickly assimilated themselves into the process. In a word, the problem statement they had written said *SPEED* or, more to the point, the lack of it. Pricing wasn't the only issue suffering from a lack of speed and the resulting inefficiency and dissatisfaction. Bringing new products to market and dealing with customer complaints or customer inquiries led the list of things that were bogged down and incredibly slow and unresponsive. The root cause was the churn and "elevator" decision-making processes. Harry, at one point, saw where this was going and almost bailed out. He saw his own face emerging like a watermark behind the written problem statement as it was being developed. Harry sat listening as the meeting drew closer to the end, and realized that these people could have really clobbered him if they had wanted to, but they didn't. They weren't attacking him; they were attacking the process.

At the end, Harry reflected these thoughts to the entire group.

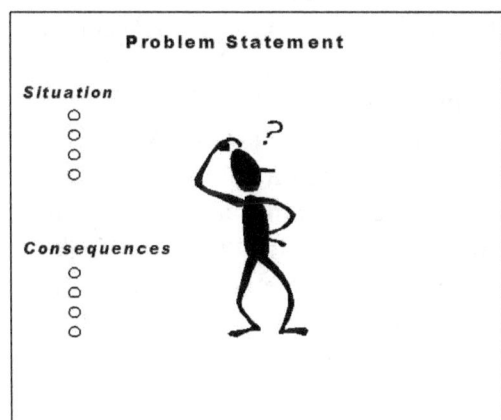

He said it had been a long time since he had felt this exhausted, yet this good. He recognized how much a part of the problem he was, but made a commitment that he would be an even bigger part of the solution. He went on to say that it was clear that the decision-making processes of Harry's Haggle Corp. were no longer competitive. "But," Harry said, "Let's stick with this process and get back together tomorrow and work through to Shared Aims and an Action Plan we all own." Of all the Stories that would be told in Harry's Haggle Corp. in the years to come, this would be an all-time favorite. Harry had just righted the "Harry's Haggle

Corp. Boat." Harry and the team had learned how to challenge what people do without attacking and challenging the value of the person. It was an important lesson, and one the Haggle Corporation would learn to leverage.

## *"I wan'na be just like Mike!"*

Benchmarking is a very effective leadership-challenging tool. Benchmarking seeks out the best-of-the-best, no matter where it is or what industry or sector it is in. Benchmarking is not *baselining*. Staying in your own class or industry or sector and looking for "who is best at what we do" isn't benchmarking. Baselining is competitive analysis and comparison. There is definitely a place and purpose for it, but its focus is on what is and what should be, and on current practices of competition and expectations of customers. If you use baselining to "aim your cannons," you're generally taking aim at the caboose of a speeding train.

Benchmarking gets an organization to break the mold and look at what *could be*. It gives insight into a "class" of competition. In athletics, there are a range of performance classes, from "recreational" to world-class. If you happen to be in a "recreational league," when it comes to competition and expectations, is winning being a better "recreational" competitor? Benchmarking sets the standards at the highest level and challenges you with "Why not!" What's the leverage of being a better recreational player, versus acquiring world-class attributes and continuing to play against recreational competitors? Everyone wants to be "just like Mike" when it comes to basketball. The same is true for organizations. Every organization wants to be the best, but few get there. Benchmarking is the path that will challenge and lead those who can make the commitment.

## *Stealing with Pride*

Benchmarking seeks out not only what is done and its results, but also searches for and provides an in-depth analysis of *how* an organization goes about doing it. Benchmarking seeks out best practices, no matter where they are. Full-blown benchmarking can be an expensive, time-consuming, resource-depleting process. Some organizations steer away from benchmarking completely because they feel that they don't have deep enough pockets. Fifteen or twenty years ago, that might have been a valid reason for not going ahead with Benchmarking. Twenty years ago, benchmarking was a do-it-yourself proposition. It is not anymore.

Over at Arlans' General, people were really feeling energized. They were experiencing success both inside and outside of the market, and it felt good after years of being an "also ran." People were reflecting how different an organization they had become. They could look back and see how much they had changed, and what those changes had resulted in. If a little change is good, "a lot would be that much better" was becoming a prevailing attitude (albeit dangerous if not properly channeled).

A group of five people put together a proposal for benchmarking and sent it to Billy Bob, asking for a "sit." Billy Bob called them back the next day and asked them to come right on up. There was a lot of excitement as the five swept into Billy Bob's office. Billy Bob opened by saying how much he liked their idea for benchmarking, and how he too felt the time was right. "We need to really get out of our box and challenge ourselves. We've learned to walk, and now it's time to see how to do it best!" Billy Bob said. He went on to say, "I wish we had all the resources to carry out your entire proposal. The fact is that we don't." What the team had put together was heavy with travel. One in the group later reflected, "It looked like an industrial tourist brochure."

Billy Bob scratched up on the board the process shown here. "Surf the Web and the libraries, and see what's out there." Billy Bob said, "I think we'll all be surprised." With that, the team sallied forth and hit the Web and the university and public libraries. They found there was already a ton of material out there, waiting for those who came looking. They were surprised at how available and complete it was. They came back with more ideas on best practices and measures than they could handle. Two weeks later, they were back in Billy Bob's office, relating what they found and their analysis. With that, Billy Bob said, "It's time we took this to the PLT."

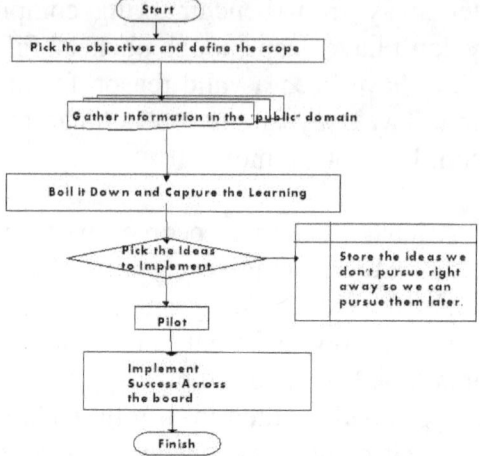

Benchmarking establishes what world-class means – simply the highest class of performance. But more importantly, it sets the course, gives the compass, and challenges others to get there. Putting your organization's own practices, behaviors, and results up against the best is a *challenging* method that can produce dramatic results. Organizations don't need "deep pockets" to get started. Take what is already out there and openly available. "Stealing with pride" isn't theft. It's getting over the "not-invented-here" syndrome that seems to be such a pervasive barrier.

## "WHAT IF ...?"

A very simple but effective *challenging* behavior is asking and seeking the answer to the question of WHAT IF? It puts your organization and its pursuits into an entirely different frame. It confronts potentialities while time is still on your side. There are three ways decisions get made. You can make them, someone else can make them for you, or time can take away possible choices to the extent that there is only one "choice" left, which by definition isn't a choice at all.

Over at Higgles Power Zone Inc., El had given "BA" and Jim Spin a "significant emotional event." El had provided an instant replay of their behavior that could only be read one way. Both "BA" and Jim concluded that they had opened up so many fronts that it was draining and confusing the organization. Projects people were going ahead with weren't getting done well. The confusion had to stop.

So, "BA" got the entire senior staff together and explained how he saw it. Being the first to say everything was messed up made it easy for everyone to get on board. "BA" said, "We haven't made the choices we need to make that will get us to where we want to go." He added, "In effect we said YES to everything. We've got to start saying NO." Everyone quickly agreed, but then the battle about whose projects were going to get axed ensued. "BA" listened quietly, and watched and listened as the battle escalated. He finally intervened. He said that he hadn't heard one thing advocated that he didn't want to say yes to, but the problem still was ". . . what are the few things we are going to say YES to and all make a commitment to see through before we start something else?"

Jim Spin advanced the idea that they ought to develop each of the *solution* ideas people had and put some resources needed next to each. After that was done, "Let's ask the question **WHAT IF** for each of them, and determine the benefits and impact each of these would have on our competitive position *if* we went ahead and did them." Simplicity has elegance.

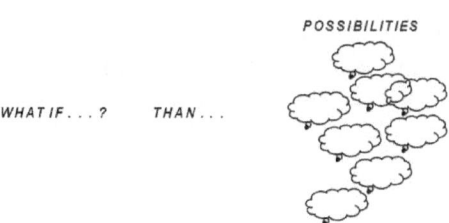

They quickly got to the task at hand and ranked the list of solutions according to the value and benefits each would provide (highest to lowest). They then ranked the same solutions in terms of resources needed (highest to lowest). When they put them side by side, the answer to which way to go began to emerge. By the time they had completed combining and deleting some of the solutions (there was an inherent overlap and synergy in doing some together), they had a short list in hand. Being action-oriented, they were ready to roll into action.

But Jim Spin, burnt once, was now the wiser. He said, "Before we go running out the door, let's ask the question WHAT IF again. IF we unleash our new understanding on the organization without anything else to support it, WHAT will be the organization's reaction?" That stopped everyone cold. Just going out and "blurting" what they had just decided wasn't going to produce a much different outcome than the Revival Rally had, except in the opposite direction. They weren't done asking What If. "BA" reflected that: "Maybe we ought to give El the key to this conference room and tell her not to let us out until we can answer every What If. We're killing ourselves with our good intentions if we don't." From that day forward, asking the question *WHAT IF* became a religion at Higgles Power Zone Inc. It became a powerful forward-looking tool not only for challenging implementing solutions, but also for looking into the competitive market and divining and quantifying possibilities for innovation, and for sorting out those things that would be of little benefit or use.

## *"WHY, WHY . . . WHY?"*

If there were a word in the English language that could be cited as the agreed upon #1 leader in parental frustration, it would be the word WHY. "WHY?" is a question children ask instinctively and repetitively in their quest to learn. It is also a word that, in time, is generally discouraged and many times ignored (particularly when children hit their teen years). So, it isn't too much of a stretch to figure out why "grown-ups" don't ask it very often.

"WHY?" is a *challenging* word. It asks for an accounting. It calls for explanation. TOYOTA Motor Company institutionalized *challenging* through asking and answering the question WHY. Toyota has been benchmarked as a leader in employee suggestions. A best practice that has been noted is their looking at *outcomes* and seeking the answer to why. Why did it happen this way? They don't stop after asking it and answering it once, but they keep on asking it until it doesn't make sense to ask again. Some have coined it the **5W**

**process**. When looking at a situation or problem, ask and answer the question why five times.

In practice, seldom does the process get to or beyond five times before it makes no sense to ask why again. What the process seeks is **root cause**. If *why* is only asked once or twice, an organization will typically have in hand the immediate cause. Immediate cause is important in problem solving because it's what must be known to "stop the bleeding." But if an organization halts there, it leaves the door open for recurrence. The work to establish the root cause is directed at finding and eliminating the pathway for the same problem to raise its head again in the future.

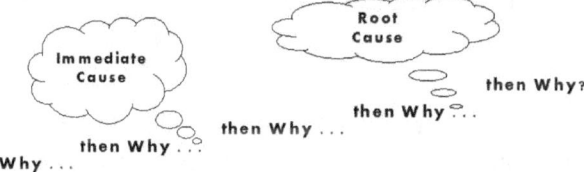

Willie at Wiggles Lawn Ornaments got into the **5W** process when a shipment was missed and the customer called him, really upset. "Outdoor Christmas decorations only sell at Christmas time. If I don't get my order in two days, don't bother sending it at all!" Willie asked the first person he saw to "go out there and find out why the order hadn't shipped." A short time later, the person came back with the revelation that the order was palletized in the warehouse, but shipping papers hadn't been cut yet. Willie told them to get the papers cut and get the shipment on the road by that night.

After the dust settled, Willie got the people "in the know" together in the conference room. Willie said, "Something's bothering me about that order. Let's reconstruct what we know." Willie used the **5W** process. It didn't get beyond four. What they all discovered was that they had a policy that made perfect sense from the viewpoint of the *ownership* stakeholders, but was at cross purposes with *customers'* needs and values. The cost weighting on their scoreboard got them again, but the fix was easy. An *if/then* statement was placed into Wiggly Lawn Ornaments Inc.'s order entry and fulfillment software system that would ensure that this didn't crop up again. If Willie had not taken this problem to the ground and challenged the organization with WHY, it would be a sure thing that Wiggly Lawn Ornaments Inc. would be seeing and solving the same immediate problem over and over again, but maybe not. Maybe customers would find a different supplier for special delivery needs.

## *Feeling the Force*

**Challenging** can be exhilarating and enabling, or it can be demoralizing and incapacitating. Leadership behavior around challenging sets the tone and the agenda. The voice that leads is loud and powerful. If challenging is deployed by leadership like a broadax, there is neither a question about what to expect from the organization in terms of their response, nor how challenging will be emulated and cascade down throughout the organization.

Collaborative challenging is a world-class practice. It seeks out knowledge. It is the foundation of a learning organization. Non-collaborative challenging closes the door to learning. It puts people on the defensive, so the truth will never be known. Collaborative challenging always seeks out what COULD BE, and doesn't get mired in justifying and defending the status quo!

# CHAPTER VIII – To *CHANNEL*

"A tough decision is when you can only say **yes** to a few from among many great options; and must say **no** to all the others."

| | The verbs of Change - CHANNEL |
|---|---|
| *Verb* | to form; to convey or direct into |
| *Noun* | the bed where a natural stream of water runs |

To CHANNEL is a delicate business. There aren't many things more destructive than a river that has come out of its banks. At the same time, there are few things more creative than a river out of its banks remaking and recasting the terrain that once defined it. CHANNELING the energy of an organization is analogous to harnessing the power of a river through the use of a dam or diversion, and transferring the river's capacity to create through an electric turbine and transmission lines to the "point-of-attack."

Fooling with "Mother Nature" is chancy. So is channeling. The issue with both is too . . . too much, little, many, few, wide, narrow, long, short, etc. *Channeling* is difficult and demanding work. Diligence here separates the frontrunners from the "also running." Channeling is about picking the right objectives (the first principle of warfare). It is at the core of any improvement process. You just can't say YES to everything, although some try. But, saying no to the wrong things can have similar outcomes. No matter what size the organization is or how small a piece of a larger organization one looks at, there are always more opportunities than resources to go around. The effective deployment of limited resources is the nature of channeling. The guiding principle of channeling is ***BE***

***DRIVEN BY FACTS***. You'll never have all the facts. If you did, a decision wouldn't have to be made. What to do would be obvious. However, the *more* facts your decisions and choices are based on, the better the outcomes.

Measuring is an integral part of effective channeling. Without it, you find yourself running in a fog. It removes the shroud of subjectivity. Measuring may be the most strategic thing organizations do. On a practical level, it defines the organization. What an organization measures determines the problems it sees. The problems an organization sees determines the solutions it picks. The solutions it picks to implement determines what it does. What an organization does defines what it is!

### *Sharpen the blade!*

Back at Higgles Power Zone Inc., "BA" et al. had gotten a discipline into the organization that had been missing. The "What IF" religion had begun to pay off. The leadership's choices were being acted on and the "What IF" had been extended to contingency planning. They were also discovering that they weren't systematic enough about evaluating opportunities. They had made a big step using the What If approach to rein back the practice of saying yes to everything that the Revival Rally had unleashed. But, "BA" felt they needed to get better. Along the way, they had started working on a Leadership Process. At their Friday staff meeting, "BA" said, "We have to figure out a better way to do the What & What Order block of work. We really don't have a disciplined process. I think there is an opportunity, but I'm not sure how to get at it."

## The LEADERSHIP PROCESS

|  | CHOOSING | PLANNING | DOING |
|---|---|---|---|
| **TARGET** | What the entity aspires to BE & DO in its future state. | WHAT & WHAT ORDER things need to get done in order to progress toward the future defined. | Determine the changes and lead the shifts that must take place to ensure success. |
| **ALIGN** | Aligned BEHAVIORAL PRINCIPLES that will guide it. | Aligned PLANS that can be acted on that provide order. | Aligned EFFORT. |
| **IMPLEMENT** | Securing the resources, and audit the overall progress and on-going correctness of the aspiration. | Roll out the PLANS and allocate the resources; audit the effectiveness and efficiency of the plans as delivered. | Deploy the resources and audit the effort. GETTING IT DONE! |

Jim Spin had gone back to school after El's enlightenment about not having their act together. The short courses and books he'd picked up were rich with tools, but he'd been uncomfortable about pulling them out. This looked like the right time and place, so he gave a pitch for using the Criteria Rating process to help with their dilemma. Everyone had seen it before, and some had experience with it, so it was an easy sell. But that was the last *easy* step.

The Criteria Rating process was straightforward enough. Pick your options and then rate each one against a set of criteria, giving them a score of 1-5 for each criterion, where 5 equates to the most or best and 1 equals the worst or least. At the end, add the columns up. The highest, in theory, ought to be the top priority, and so forth. They had, in some manner, done this when they ranked their choices using values, benefits, and resources. But, when they came to getting specific about the *criteria* that would channel their thinking, they discovered that they were miles apart on a consensus.

Getting into more details around the values they were going to move forward with and how these values would shape their offerings to each of the stakeholders brought to light an issue central to their success: leadership alignment. At a high philosophical level, there was leadership alignment. But, when it got to a pragmatic level, defining what those philosophies mean in terms of actions and the expectations around them, they weren't anywhere near aligned. The **bells** an organization hears are the high level philosophies (the leadership's composite statement of their beliefs). Leadership actions on the practical level around those philosophies are the **voices** organizations listen to and channel their responses based on. "The reason we are not sharp on the *What & What Order* block is that we weren't sharp enough on the *Choosing* column," Jim observed.

Although there was disappointment, there was also optimism. "BA" reflected that they still hadn't gotten down to the short hairs about what it was they, the leadership, were going to say yes to, and what they would say no to. "If we can't get that straight ourselves, we can't expect the organization to do any better." El's message of cleaning up their act was getting clearer.

## Focus, Focus, Focus . . .

Willie and the Wiggly Lawn Ornament team were troubled by the same issues: what to say yes to and what to say no to or put on hold. Wiggly's focus had improved tremendously as the SLT refined the Leadership Process and the channeling it provided. The Wiggly Lawn Ornaments Inc. Vision, Principles, and Strategies, along with their plans and resource deployment had all evolved as the organization cycled through the implementation and feedback processes. Core to the Wiggly Vision was growth. In one of their major product lines, they were stymied. They seemed to be doing the right things, but they weren't getting anywhere out in the market.

They had also discovered that the same simple tool deployed on the shop floor for Problem Analysis and Problem Solving was equally beneficial in channeling boardroom decisions. Willie called the struggling Product Line Team in. Together they worked through the situation using the Cause & Effect (a.k.a. Fishbone) Diagram to look at what they knew. As they went through this, the only thing that seemed to emerge was that if they wanted to grow this product line they would have to cut prices.

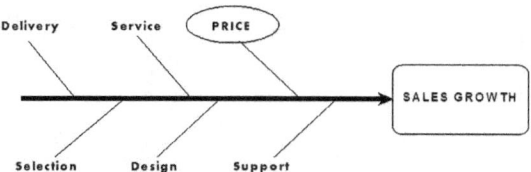

That, in turn, meant they had to cut costs. Wiggly Lawn Ornaments Inc. put a lot into their product lines. Their Vision clearly stated that they wanted to be the premier supplier in the markets they participated in. They knew they had the highest value offering on the market. Nobody beat them in terms of product design (aesthetics and durability), or in delivery, service support, or selection and breadth of choices. This product line oozed Wiggly's values.

## *"Just the facts ma'am, just the facts."*

Willie wasn't satisfied. He said, "That product line is a statement about who we are. We can't go cutting corners on materials and features. Who is ready to move on price?" The answer was nobody. When they began looking at the detail on the fishbone, their analysis was long on perceptions and feelings, and short on facts. But Price was the fulcrum, so a Task Team was chartered to quickly go after and bring back "the FACTS."

Two weeks later, the Product Line Team and Willie reconvened to review what the Task Team had uncovered. The Task Team presented the following. Their fact-finding mission disclosed two very distinct segments of customers. Competitors A, B, and C were locked into the first, and Wiggly Lawn Ornaments Inc. owned the second. What's more, with all the recent improvements that had been made with this product line, from design to service, the added value had pushed them off the Fair Value Line to the delight of the customers who made up this higher value segment. Many customers remarked that they were pleased "Wiggly has held the line on price increases." The Task Team finished their presentation by saying that, with regard to price, "If anything, we ought to be raising price by 10%, not cutting it."

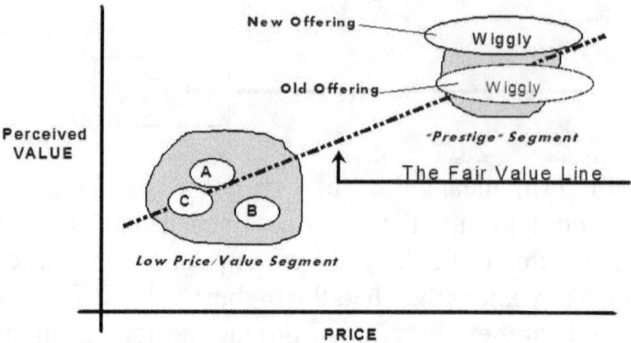

The facts were clear. In order to compete with A-C, prices would have to roll back 40%. Even then, Wiggly Lawn Ornaments Inc. might only be marginally successful because the people who were buying those products sometimes only wanted them for a one-time use (a party or special occasion). Competition wasn't going to sit still either. They would probably roll their prices back further in response to Wiggly Lawn Ornaments Inc.'s entry. The Task Team also observed that Wiggly might lose their existing customers because now "everyone would have a Wiggly product on their lawn." Owning a Wiggly lawn ornament, it turned out, was a status statement.

What started out as relatively *simple* had become quite complex. Cutting the price was, for now, off the table, but bringing out a new product line to compete in the segment at the Lower Price/Value level had far-reaching implications. This new offering would clearly be outside of the Business Definition in the Wiggly Lawn Ornaments Inc. Vision (Values, Offerings, and Segments). If Willie were to say YES, he would also have to say YES to a new business definition, and to the diversion of substantial resources away from other efforts to support it. Willie concluded by saying, "You've got the ball on where to go from here on pricing. That's your decision. But chasing into this new segment you have identified is outside our business definition. That's an SLT issue, and I'll take it from here."

Willie and Wiggly Lawn Ornaments Inc. had experienced the value of digging up a few more facts to facilitate channeling their focus. Some might have reacted against the Task Team's chartering, and countered with the old but *true* adage of Paralysis by Analysis. There are never enough facts, but when is enough, enough? There aren't any formulas, but if you find yourselves revisiting the same data, only repackaged into different forms, you are probably experiencing Analysis by Paralysis. Going out for more data for absorption into the same analysis process is not Analysis by Paralysis. Trading off time to find facts is a difficult part of the channeling process. The answer lies within the *time context* of the decision. When will *time* remove *which choices* from consideration?

## *What Now?*

At Harry's Haggle Corp., Harry Huckster had been challenged by the revelation that he was the problem. He had accepted that reality, but Harry also recognized that he was the solution. Harry assembled the Leadership Team and said, "We've got to go back to school and learn how to compete." During a visit to Wiggly Lawn Ornaments, his old friend Willie had given him their current competitive supplier analysis that the Supplier Improvement Process Team had developed. Harry said, "It isn't just Wiggly that is doing this. This isn't an isolated event. The rules have changed. We need to figure out how to play, and what's more, how to win." Everyone knew the bottom line verified what Harry was saying.

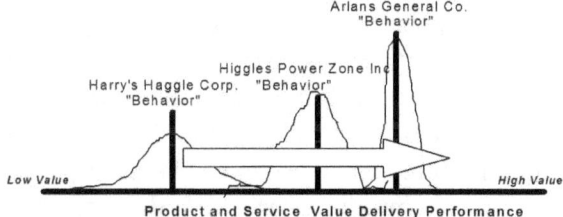

As competitors had reshaped their offerings with increased value, Harry's Haggle Corp. had to give ground on price. Harry went on to say, "We're behind on this, but we still have time. Arlans' General is definitely the customer satisfaction leader and is taking share from us and from Higgles Power Zone Inc. Higgles is getting their act together and battling back. We need to act, but we need to channel our resources and act deliberately." With that, a heated debate broke out as to which way to go and what things to do.

Harry intervened. "We've been arrogant, plain, and simple. We need to get to the bottom of what this picture Wiggly Lawn Ornaments Inc. has given to us means. We're going to use the Communications Process to focus us, and we're going to figure out exactly how we stack up." The team quickly arrived at an agenda to pursue. They put themselves in a military context focused on strengths and weaknesses: where and how competitors were attacking, and where and how they were most likely to attack again. One sub team looked at Higgles Power Zone Inc. and Arlans' General; the other team would look at themselves.

### *Concrete feet ain't all bad!*

When the analysis was finished, they learned that their strengths were their technology and assets. One thing they had done well was continually renewing their assets. The Harry's Haggle Corp. people were strength and, when combined with their assets, their internal operations were the best. Their weakness was in their connection with their customers. The approaches and their processes were insensitive and uncooperative, much less collaborative. Arlans' General's strength was their collaboration and the flexibility and speed with which they made product line changes and innovations, and Higgles Power Zone Inc. was catching up. But, neither Arlans' General nor Higgles Power Zone Inc. were as strong when it came to technology or the competitiveness of their assets. They were running on older technology, and the volume, particularly at Arlans' General, had to be keeping them just above the breakeven point. One customer summed it up this way for them: "With respect to what you offer, the quality of your product designs and conformance to them is without a doubt the best. But, you're too slow, and just not adapting with us to where our markets and customers are taking us."

Harry and the team thought about it. The analysis had given them insights they hadn't had before. They continued to work through the Communications Process, and quickly came to Shared Aims and an Action Plan they all owned. Their strategy wasn't that complex.

Simply put, stick with our strengths (our assets and technology), and continue to strengthen them. Use the Strengthened Assets with the already strong but underutilized Human Resources to drive to the lowest cost producer. While that was underway, go out and figure out what customers really want and how they want to "do business," and redefine how a supplier should behave. You win from your strengths. They'd made the right technology and investment decisions over the years. Their "concrete feet" were that, but they were more than just that. Their concrete feet were also a **concrete barrier**. Higgles Power Zone Inc. and Arlans' General would have to make some serious cash outlays and boost up their process engineering to catch them, and that would take a whole lot more time than it would for Harry's Haggle Corp. to become "user friendly." Harry's Haggle Corp. had just gotten focus. They knew now where to channel their effort.

## *Channeling is Focus.*

In a competitive environment, focus may not be everything, but it is a common attribute of winners. From athletics, to education, to industry, focus is always cited when the winners are interviewed. Organizational leadership has to think of focus in the same way they would think of an optical system. There is a lot of parallelism. An out of focus optical system produces lousy results, regardless of the quality of the optics. Similarly, many organizations continue to seek out, purchase, or develop better "optics," and are continually disappointed with the results. There are a number of instances where competitors entered the fray with substantially inferior "optics," yet managed to outperform everyone else. The determinant is focus.

*Channeling* is the focusing process of an organization. It's an essential leadership behavior. Trying to be all things to everyone, or do all things that are good, is counterproductive. The interest and excitement around core competencies some time back dealt with focus, or more to the point, where to channel the organization's energy.

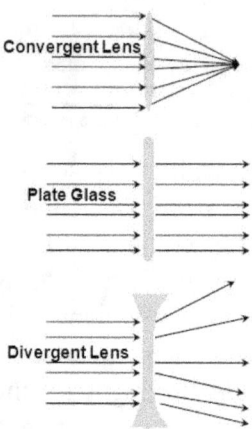

The *channeling* process of leadership can be thought of as a lens. There are a variety of lenses. Some cause the light incident on them to converge; some cause the light to diverge; and others just let it pass through. The light in this analogy can be the energy of the organization. It might be the bombardment of information and data impinging on the organization. Or, it might be an array of ideas or suggestions. Whether it's one or all, the role of leadership and leadership process is to channel these and focus them. The act and process of channeling is the convergent lens of an organization.

The *Leadership Process* is the master *channeling process* of an organization. Each of the nine blocks of work consecutively refines the focus and concentration of what and how things are and will be done. The lens can be a person, or it can engage the entire resources of the organization.

## The LEADERSHIP PROCESS

|  | CHOOSING | PLANNING | DOING |
|---|---|---|---|
| **TARGET** | What the entity aspires to BE & DO in its future state. | WHAT & WHAT ORDER things need to get done in order to progress toward the future defined. | Determine the changes and lead the shifts that must take place to ensure success. |
| **ALIGN** | Aligned BEHAVIORIAL PRINCIPLES that will guide it. | Aligned PLANS that can be acted on that provide order. | Aligned EFFORT. |
| **IMPLEMENT** | Securing the resources, and audit the overall progress and on-going correctness of the aspiration. | Roll out the PLANS and allocate the resources; audit the effectiveness and efficiency of the plans as delivered. | Deploy the resources and audit the effort. GETTING IT DONE! |

Every organization can reflect on their Leadership Process and find any of the three analogous lens forms. In fact, effective Leadership Processes have all three types of lenses present and active. Channeling is in fact a sequence of diverging and converging analysis and decision making. In the Leadership Process model, the flow is divergent to convergent, top to bottom, and left to right. The process diverges and seeks out the broadest range of possibilities in the Targeting Row and converges to the few in the Implementation Row. The Choosing column diverges and sets the boundaries for the organization as wide as possible, and then converges down to action in the Doing column.

### *"That was quick!"*

At Arlans' General, Jim Bob and the Benchmarking Proposal Team brought their package into the PLT for review. The knowledge they had gained about best practices and possibilities really expanded the field of choices. There wasn't one idea that the Benchmarking Team brought in that the PLT didn't wish they had done yesterday. The ideas laid out were exciting. But, it was like a brain dump. There were fifteen best practice ideas in all.

The PLT had made a point to learn how to use the tools that they had picked up from courses they had attended and books they had read. They reasoned that the more tools they had and knew how to use, the more effective they would be. After a short discussion, they decided to use the *N/3* tool, and invited Jim Bob and the team to participate with them.

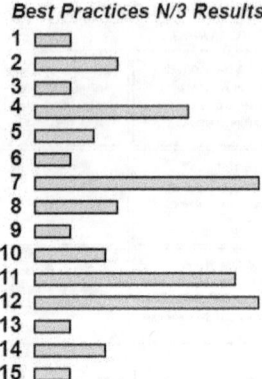

N/3 is a narrowing or convergence tool. Very simply, you divide the number of possibilities generated by three and then that's how many "votes" each member involved has to cast for their preferences. You're not voting for or against an item. You're just stating which, in your opinion, are more equal, your preference of order (the first to third to pursue).

In this case, everyone had five picks. When the results were tallied, a pattern emerged. There were four ideas that were, after a short discussion, consensus all-star ideas. But, after another discussion, it was obvious that the resources weren't available to pursue all of them simultaneously. They would have to converge again. This time they used the Criteria Rating Process. In the end, one best practice emerged as the dominant leader to move forward with at the present time. With that decision in hand, the PLT began the process of integrating it into the Strategic Plan. It wasn't so much "What" as it was "How" that they had all felt was missing.

## *"This doesn't feel right."*

People using "process tools" to channel (like Criteria Rating and N/3) feel uncomfortable in many instances. The cause of the discomfort is important to root out. It might lie in the fact that the choices or options weren't developed fully enough, in which case it should stop there until more detail can be obtained. It might be personal (my idea lost), in which case a person usually had some baggage they failed to check and disclose before the process started.

It might also be that the list of choices wasn't divergent enough. In that case, the time should be taken to expand it. Whatever the case, discomfort, if it's present, ought to be put on the table and understood. In many cases, when people are new to using tools like these in a channeling process, the discomfort is coming from the speed at which a convergence was accomplished. Decisions that took days or months in the past are made in hours. There can be a pervasive feeling that this is too good to be true, that something must be wrong. If that feeling emerges, test it. The tools will never be valuable until there is a shared level of confidence in them.

## *Feeling the FORCE*

It's hard to get a sense of the energy of a river while you're tube floating down a placid stretch. However, there is no escaping how powerful the river really is if you try to stand under the spillway of a dam. Channeling is a leadership behavior that continually seeks out the power that is resident in organizations and concentrates it where it will do the most good. Channeling is not only a behavior, but it's also a process. The better the process is, the better the product and the results will be. Identifying and concentrating on improving the channeling processes throughout an organization can pay big dividends, but it isn't easy. Channeling is order. Order is paid for with freedom. Channeling is saying yes, but it also is saying no. There are a number of tools to help.

# CHAPTER IX – To *CHAMPION*

"What a person does speaks so loudly, it's impossible to hear what they say!"

> ***The verbs of Change - CHAMPION***
> ***Verb*** to protect or fight for as a champion; to act as a militant supporter of
>
> ***Noun*** a warrior or fighter; a militant advocate or defender; one that does battle for another's rights or honor

To CHAMPION is to risk. The naysayer risks nothing. If things don't work out, "I told you so." If they do work out, "You didn't understand what I was saying!" On the other hand, when you are *for* something, there is a downside. You might be wrong, or what you are for and championing might be right, but if implemented poorly, the results are as good as being wrong.

Effective championing has a lot to do with timing. A would-be champion can have all the right notions and strategies, but if the timing isn't right, and the resistance and barriers to the change being championed cannot be dealt with, advancing a position transcends risk and moves into the arena of chance. Conversely, if the timing is right and the organizational energy has moved from resistance to support, that's not really championing. It's doing the obvious.

Championing is moving an idea or concept forward in a way that manages the risks, and confronts and deals with the barriers and resistance to change. Championing isn't bossing and it isn't managing. Championing is leading. There are some things that can only be "managed," and there are other things that can only be "bossed," but improvement can only be led. Championing isn't reserved only to certain positions or titles. However, those who might champion can take some simple lessons from the different roles and styles of hierarchical leaders. The three basic styles are shown here. If you're *not living* in the right hand column (Leading), you're not championing – you're generally just creating a lot of counterproductive hullabaloo around "new ideas and directions."

| | Leadership Role Behavior Choices | | |
|---|---|---|---|
| | BOSSING | MANAGING | LEADING |
| **BEHAVIOR** | | | |
| Style | Directing Activities | Setting Objectives | Provide Vision |
| Generating Energy | Pushing | Pulling | Creating Ownership |
| Channeling | Disciplining | Critique to Standards | Audit for Upgrade |
| Boundary Setting | Maintaining | Testing | Expanding |
| **RESULTS** | | | |
| Mental Space | Obedience to me | Alternate Methods | Alternate Outcomes |
| Mode of Behavior | Reactive | Ego | Purposeful |
| **DEGREE of CHANGE** | NONE | INCREMENTAL | STEP-CHANGE |
| **GOAL** | What Is | What Should Be | What Could Be |

All great leaders are champions. All those who champion are not great leaders. The ability to keep that which you champion in context, the perceived presence of those involved, is the key determinant of success. If people don't or can't understand the meaning and significance of that which you champion, there will be 0% support and 100% resistance.

Before going out to champion, one should get a "booster shot" of HUMILITY. Humility is not meekness. Humility is the ability to see reality as it is and accept it as the starting point of your journey. And, while on the improvement journey, it is the ability to stay in contact with the ground, what's really happening, not what you hope or would like to be happening.

As the saying goes, "If you want to manage something, manage yourself!" When you get into championing, you're into high gear, so extra diligence is called for, particularly with respect to managing your own behavior. The other prerequisite to championing, in addition to humility, is MATURITY. Maturity is the ability to self-manage your personal thinking and behavior in a way that your courage and consideration for others are continually balanced. The bolder the ideas and concepts championed, the greater the courage and the greater the consideration that is needed.

Those would-be champions, who don't sense the reality of the timing of an idea or the resistance toward it, lack humility. Those that courageously move forward with bold ideas, lacking consideration for the people who the changes will impact, have a maturity deficiency. Great champions, just as great leaders, have high quotients of both humility and maturity.

Effective champions are always seen and understood as serving the purposes of the organization being impacted, and not the purposes of the person who is championing. Championing is purposeful and selfless behavior. If the person championing is perceived as serving his/her self interest, the resistance to change will be insurmountable.

True champions are those who not only ring loud bells, but also keep their voices and stories well-aligned with that which they champion. Those people whose voices and stories are misaligned with the new directions being championed must work overtime to correct this deficiency. Neglecting this aspect will only lead to sluggishness and complacency in the organization, as well as challenges to one's personal integrity.

There are a few touchstones that those engaged in championing ought to continually revisit and assess. They are

*Clarity*, *Resistance*, *Commitment*, and *Involvement*. These four are very much interdependent and reciprocally maintain each other.

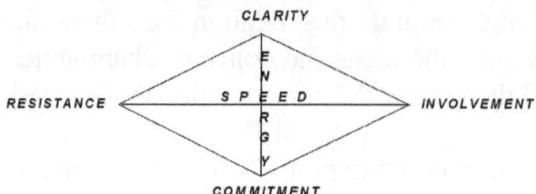

*Clarity* in this context is about expectations. Are the objectives and results clear and understandable? Is there a clear sense of how things will look and feel differently after the improvement being championed is completed? Without that in place, how can there be ownership or commitment, or how can you speak to resistance, or how can one achieve involvement of people outside of themselves or their tight circle of influence?

*Resistance* is reality. When you are championing a change, there is always going to be resistance, first from within oneself, and then from the organization as a whole. Not seeking out and putting resistance up on the table and dealing with it only fuels more resistance. The higher the resistance, the murkier what is being championed becomes, and the less willing people are to become involved, much less take ownership in the changes being championed.

*Commitment* is resolve. Many instances of setbacks and failures arise from a lack of leadership resolve to continue on after sensing resistance or experiencing adverse or unplanned for outcomes. Who's going to get involved with, or have ownership in, or not be outright resistant to something, no matter how clear, that lacks the leadership resolve to follow through?

*Involvement* is ownership. People get involved with what they own. The thrill of invention isn't reserved solely for Einstein or for a person having an original insight. Everyone that follows, when they break through their mental blocks and see and understand the invention of another for the first time, can experience it. When they do, they get involved. Involvement enhances clarity, extinguishes resistance, and builds commitment.

Commitment and Clarity throttle the organizational *energy* generated for that which is championed. Resistance and Involvement are the regulators of organizational *speed* around improvements being championed. The more clarity and commitment around that which is being championed, the more energy there is for making the necessary changes. The lower the resistance and the higher the involvement, the faster the organization can move to the improved state being championed. Championing isn't loud, bold proclamations. It isn't cheerleading on the sidelines. Championing is about being out on the playing field, hard work, sweat, and long hours.

### *How did I get into this mess, Ollie?*

Back at Arlans' General, the PLT had integrated the deployment of the selected Best Practice into their Strategic Plan. The PLT had also moved the core members of the Benchmark Team into a newly-chartered team accountable for rolling out and integrating the best practice selected across the board at Arlans' General. When the full Best Practice Team assembled, they quickly learned that none of them had the line authority to just go out and do it. The authority defined in their charter spoke to facilitating, coaching, and training. The resources available were the allocation of nominally 50% of each member's time to the task. The expectations, results, and benefits were almost verbatim what the Benchmarking team had presented. One member reflected out loud, "I wonder whether this Charter will self-destruct in 30 seconds? This looks like a mission impossible to me!" After a brief amount of discussion, they decided to get Billy Bob in here and ". . . renegotiate the terms of the Charter."

Billy Bob came in right away. After listening to the concerns, Billy Bob said that they needed to step back and look at what they were trying to do. He said, "You don't DO a best practice to an organization. If you could, we more than likely would hire someone to come in and do it to us.

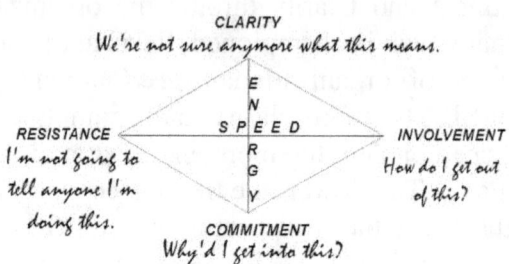

A best practice is something an organization not only does, but does to itself." Billy Bob went on to say, "Everyone remembers bad leaders and good leaders. *Great* leaders, though, are those people who, when the task is over, allow the organization to reflect and say we did it ourselves. The PLT and I want this team to be *great* leaders. When this best practice is fully integrated, the people of Arlans' General will say we did it ourselves. In short," Billy Bob said, "we want you all to first learn about, and then become, Champions." After some more discussion, Billy Bob left the team to find their way with the Championing Tetrad.

The next thing that was apparent to the team was that there was a genuine lack of clarity among them about what this best practice was really about. The concept was clear enough, but when they tried to answer questions like what the objective was for doing this, and how exactly things would look after the change, and what people would be doing differently, there positively wasn't a whole lot of clarity. After some more discussion, everyone in the room was beginning to wonder why they had gotten involved in this in the first place. When they sat back and audited where they were with the Championing Tetrad, they found the following:

Openness wasn't an issue at Arlans' General, and it was lucky for them that it wasn't. What they realized from the above was that the first step of championing is developing their own personal clarity about the improvement they would be championing. After that, they had to tackle their own resistance and barriers to commitment and involvement before they went further and tried to engage the organization as a whole. There was no doubt that this best practice was a good idea, and that integrating it into the organization was well-intentioned. But, as one team member reflected, "The pathway to hell is paved with good intentions, and if we try to go much further with this, beyond those of us in this room, we'll be walking into our own personal hell." With that bit of insight and shared awareness, they quickly went to work on a path forward that was front end loaded with building their own team understanding, clarity, and commitment, and dealing with disposing of the team's resistance first.

### *You've got to undo what you did before you can do what you've got to do.*

Joe "BA" Hurang, CEO of Higgles Power Zone Inc., had stumbled over the pitfall of *clarity* when he unleashed the Revival Rally. Only completing the first block of work in the Choosing column and going right to action had been a disaster, but it was one they could learn from. El had confronted them with a mirror, and nobody liked the image they saw. "BA" and staff were now diligently engaged in doing the work of the Choosing Column in the Leadership Work Process. They had come a long way, but more importantly, they recognized that what they were undertaking didn't have an end. Leadership is a continuum of effort, auditing, and upgrading.

When they had revisited and refined the Choosing Column work, the "What and What Order" block of work fell into place easily. From there, they rolled out into tactical plans and into implementation. They soon discovered that there was a huge amount of organizational resistance to the improvements they were trying to advance. "BA" was frustrated. "Why aren't people getting involved in this, and why all the pushback?" There was a quick round of seconding that emotion. The facts were clear. They'd done a good job of basing their decisions on cold, hard facts and statistics, and "By golly, every one of us is committed," someone else chimed in.

"Why is there such a wait and see attitude out there. Why won't people grab hold?" "BA" went on to ruminate.

Jim Spin seized the moment. "There is a lot of energy out there to get on with our plans," Jim said. "People seem to understand what it is we need to do, and feel the commitment in this room to do it." Jim went on to say, "But, the resistance and hesitation doesn't have anything to do with the business facts around our position, competition, and customers. It has everything to do with the facts regarding what we did and what happened after the Revival Rally. We didn't demonstrate commitment through our actions; we didn't provide an avenue to deal with questions, concerns, and resistance; and the results we got were sporadic involvement at best."

"BA" was about ready to blow. "If that wasn't the lamest excuse he'd ever heard," he thought, "then they can call me Joseph!" But "BA" held his tongue, and, remembering El's words, asked Jim to help him understand.

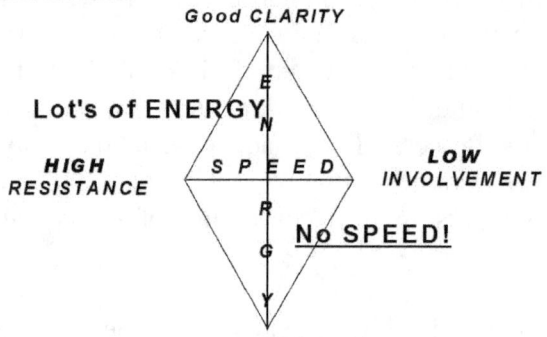

When the discussion was over, it was clear that the Revival Rally, rather than being "BA's" finest hour, had turned out to be one of his biggest busts. "We've got to close that piece of our history out before we can move on," Jim said. "Regardless of which way we go in the future or how things work out, our past is common to any eventuality that's out there." Jim concluded by saying that the reason the resistance and lack of enthusiasm was continuing was because they were acting like what happened never happened.

With dead silence in the room, "BA" stared into the top of the table, saying nothing. "BA" was staggered by what he had learned. His personal denial wasn't easy to overcome, but he finally did. "The barrier is me, plain and simple," he said. "I've really been avoiding dealing with the reality of the Revival Rally and the confusion that it generated. I went out to champion what I believe is right and I blew it. That's the bad news. The good news is that there is definitely plenty of energy out there to get on with it." He continued, "I got us into this and I have to get us out. Let's schedule another rally, but this time we will call it the *Reality Rally*. I've learned a lot about change and what championing means, and so has everyone in this organization. It's time to *leverage* it." "BA" and Higgles Power Zone Inc. had come to another turning point, and had successfully navigated through a treacherous channel to open water again. This event would become an important story about "BA," who, in pretty quick order, shed the label "BA." It took a lot of courage and humility to go out and undo what he had done. But the new "Joe" pulled it off with flying colors. Joe was a changed leader, and so was Higgles Power Zone.

### *We're going too FAST!*

At Harry's Haggle Corp., Harry et al. were off and running. The Good news/Bad news about Haggle's culture was Harry. Harry was it. Everyone looked to Harry and emulated him. So, when Harry and the Leadership Team articulated their new view of Haggle's competitive position, the new customer wants and needs, and their vision and strategies to deal with them, there wasn't any hesitation. The channeling effort they had gone through and the focus and clarity they had gained left little to interpret. Harry's action, his voice, was continuing to get louder and louder. There was no question about Harry's or the Leadership Team's commitment as champions. Harry and the Leadership Team continued to expand the circle of the communications Process they had adopted, so any resistance surfaced and was resolved quickly. People were piling on and getting involved with designing and orchestrating the changes and improvements needed. Quite literally, the organization was moving at warp speed.

But all was not right. Harry was scared. He felt out of control; things were happening too fast. What had started out a few months back as an effort to off some of his personal workload had turned into a juggernaut. Three months ago, Harry had been making darn near every decision, from pricing to production schedules. Now, he was totally out of those loops. His desk used to be piled with papers for signature and action; people would be in line outside his door every morning, waiting for him to come in. Now that was all gone.

The organization had become like a person possessed. The strategies were quickly cascaded into plans and actions, and the results, Harry had to admit, were awesome. Going out to the customers and reinventing how Harry's Haggle Corp. did business reopened doors that had been closed for some time, and more than that, it was bringing in new sales. The more volume they got, the quicker the unit costs were coming down, and their "concrete feet" assets were really humming out total costs that Arlans' General or Higgles Power Zone Inc. couldn't touch.

### *The sayer of sooths says this is an omen.*

"Things are just too good," Harry thought to himself. "This is an omen." When Harry went home that night, he cornered his spouse, Martha, and explained his dilemma. He concluded by saying, "I think the company is on the brink of ruin, and the only way to save it is for me to get hold of the reins again!" to which Martha guffawed. "Harry," she said, "you've always been a control freak, and if anyone knows that, I am the one who should. But what you don't realize," she continued, "is that you're probably more in control now than you ever were before." She went on to observe that Harry was stressed out when he was doing all the work. Now he was stressed out because he wasn't doing any of the work he used to do, and the company was more successful than ever.

Before Harry could reply, Martha said, "What kind of reins are you thinking about pulling on?" Harry muttered something to the effect about taking back over the decision-making he'd been involved with before. "If you do that," Martha said, "what will people say about your commitment to what you have been out there preaching? If you go back to doing what you were doing, won't you confuse people? And if people are confused and sense you're not committed, what do you think they'll do?"

Harry didn't have anything to add. He realized Martha was right, but it still didn't feel right. Martha continued, "What sort of reins did you have on yourself? Whatever they were, they need to be handed over to the organization, and you have to figure out what kind of new reins you're going to put on yourself!" Harry knew Martha was right, again. Maybe the reins he ought to be holding were the ones that had to do with what was going on in the dynamic of the Championing Tetrad.

Harry began to doodle with the Championing Tetrad. If he went and took back over all the decision-making he'd empowered, he would be mandating a *decrease* in *involvement*. When that was

linked up with the *clarity* with which he had been articulating the direction the company needed to go, there could be no question that his personal **integrity** would be challenged, along with the integrity of everything that had been accomplished. His taking back over was an action of someone who wasn't *committed*, so doing that would for sure put a damper on the **energy effectiveness** of the organization. If he displayed a lack of *commitment*, and rescinded all that he had said in dealing with the *resistance* he had uncovered and dealt with, then how would people know what to do anymore? The self **governing** that had emerged would be extinguished and used to fuel more resistance. And with the diminishing of *clarity* and the fueling of *resistance*, people would positively lose the great sense of **intent** that had developed in recent months.

By the time the evening was over, Harry had turned himself around 180° from where he was when he had arrived home. Instead of going back to Harry's Haggle Corp. and taking back over everything he had previously been doing, Harry was going back and taking charge of increasing *clarity*, *commitment*, and *involvement*, and dealing with the *resistance* to changes as they came up and focusing on eliminating or minimizing them. Harry had just refined his role as a leader and champion.

## *The answer is sometimes right under your nose.*

Over at Wiggly Lawn Ornaments, Willie was really feeling good. It had been less than a year ago that he had been wallowing in despair over the future of the business. The company had a new focus, and people were involved and committed. A lot of things were happening and paying off with an uncanny accuracy. The bottom line was better than ever; the people of Wiggly Lawn Ornaments Inc. were enthusiastic and having fun like the old days; the community support was there; and customers had never been happier. "It just doesn't get any better than this," Willie thought to himself. But there was a rumble in the organization, a background "noise" he just couldn't put his finger on. So, on a Monday morning, he decided he'd go out and look to find out what it was.

As Willie made the rounds through the offices and shops, people were glad to see him and enthusiastic to tell him what they were doing. But, they were equally enthusiastic to tell him about what they thought should be happening. He recorded these ideas in a notebook he carried in his back pocket, and said to each and every one, "I'll get back to you." Before he went to lunch, he had twenty pages of changes and improvements that people had pointed out as "vital." After lunch, he hopped in his car and made the rounds to the outlying facilities. By the time the day was done, he had recorded almost fifty pages of ideas people wanted to pursue, and he hadn't even really seen any of the sales people yet. The rumble he had been hearing was the organization boiling up energy for new ideas like a head of steam. He realized to his dismay that there wasn't any outlet for them except "Grab Willie when you see him," and if he didn't get an outlet in place, something was going to blow.

The next day, he assembled the SLT and presented the dilemma. After a brief discussion, somebody pointed out that they had created an organization of champions. After some chuckling and banter, Willie posed the question, "But isn't that what we want?" After a bit of internalizing, the SLT converged on the same point, being: "That's exactly what we want!" This led to the next obvious question: "If that's what we want, how are we going to deal with it?"

"Grabbing Willie" was a process, but pretty lame and ineffective. Willie had promised every one of them he'd get back to them, but every one of them who'd put forward a new idea was looking for an up or down vote the next time they saw Willie, and Willie was in no way prepared to do that. One of the SLT members proposed they use the old suggestion system, ". . . after all, we already have the boxes." But, after a short dialogue, it became clear that the suggestion system in place wasn't much of a system at all, and in fact they could count on two hands the number of suggestions they'd received over the past year, so having Willie go back and tell them to put their new ideas in the suggestion box would be more of an insult than anything. Willie said they all needed to think quickly about this and reconvene later in the day to resolve it using their Communications Process.

Willie went back to his office a bit forlorn. A year ago, he was at a loss for ideas about what to do and where to go with the business. He felt the weight of that on his back, and he remembered wondering back then why he was "stuck with all this." Now, he seemed to have more "company" than he knew how to deal with. With that thought, Willie went off to lunch over at the Armadillo Grill. It was crowded as usual, but not so bad as to make him turn around and go back out the door. As he looked around, he saw things were different than the last time he had been in. The display case of "Dillo's Secret Sauces" had expanded to a whole line of offerings, from sauces to complete meals shipped overnight. There was also a grand opening banner over the entrance celebrating the opening of the fifth Armadillo Grill in a city five hundred miles down the interstate. Willie reflected to himself, "Things are really going well for Steph."

After he was seated and placed his order, Steph came over to the table and sat down. "You must be busy," she said, "I haven't seen you in a while." Willie said that things were perking over at Wiggly Lawn Ornaments Inc. too. After he gave her a condensed version of their successes, he decided he'd broach the dilemma of a company full of champions, and concluded by saying, "We need to come up with a Suggestion System that works." Steph quickly countered that he already had a system that worked. Why change it? Willie was patient. "The suggestion system we have is a joke. We got less than ten ideas last year placed in the boxes. But, it took me less than a day to get fifty pages of new ideas just walking around," Willie said. Steph replied, "That's not the system or process I was talking about. I'm talking about your Leadership Work Process. Dad said you used the same material I did to create your Leadership Process. All our suggestions, including those from customers, go right into our Leadership Process. The only trick, if you can call it that, is getting feedback into the right block of work. Look at the top row of work -- *Targets*. Every suggestion fits into one of those three blocks." With that, Steph excused herself and resumed "pressing the flesh."

Willie sat there thinking, "Dilloed again. Why didn't I think of that?" After lunch, when the meeting of the SLT reconvened, Willie introduced his insight. The SLT took the fifty pages of ideas Willie had recorded, and, sure enough, they all fit in the top row of work somewhere. At the end of the meeting, the SLT agreed that the Leadership Process was the right place for entering new ideas that people were championing. Furthermore, the people who were championing them ought to come in and be part of the process when their ideas were up for consideration. They also reflected that the SLT ought to go ferret out all the other orphan processes and systems beyond the old Suggestion System and see whether or not they fit in the Leadership Process as well.

## *Feeling the FORCE*

Societies don't build monuments to honor boo-birds, skeptics, cynics, or critics. I've yet to see a statue erected or a park named after a naysayer. Societies do build monuments for champions. They build them for people who took an idea or a concept and advanced it, despite resistance. They build monuments for people who took a risk to be *for* something and made a difference. The reason is pretty simple. Champions accomplish something. The amount of accomplishment may never be all that they had hoped for or dreamed about when they went out to champion, but as time reveals, it was significant, and altered the ways things were for the better.

Everyone has the capacity to champion. Everyone doesn't have an environment that fosters it, much less condones and celebrates it. A chronic problem of championing in an organizational setting is that the upside is a better organization, not personal gain, but the downside is the possible personal "organizational demise" of the champion. Improvement requires champions. Without someone to pick up the flag and advance it, nothing beyond the status quo will ever materialize. Champions are the messengers of the future. Shooting them is not a viable option.

An organization brimming with champions is an organization that has unparalleled energy for improvement and unequaled speed and flexibility to change and evolve itself. In short, it's an organization that, competitively, is very hard to beat. It's also a scary environment for executives who are unprepared.

# CHAPTER X – To CHECK

"Don't be fooled. Snow is frozen rain."

> ***The verbs of Change - CHECK***
> ***Verb*** to put into check; to control; to slow or bring to a stop
> ***Noun*** under restraint or control; one that arrests, limits, or restrains

Trying to stage improvement is sometimes a lot like plowing water. The water opens and boils to the steel of the plow's blade. Unfortunately, the waters are equally vigorous behind the plow as they fight to go back to where they were before disturbed. Failing to make provisions to CHECK the progress, to hold the waters back, is the root cause of most every reflective "But . . ." statement spoken.

The skill of leading has four elements – Visioning, Motivating, Order, and Audit. CHECKING is a critical task of Order and Audit. A dam is the structure, the Order that puts a river in CHECK. Auditing is the vigilance that keeps it in CHECK. While Visioning and Motivating is the plow's blade of improvement, providing a framework of Order and Auditing are what secure it.

The voices of every leader that ever lived still resonate in every venue . . . "HOLD the GAINS!" Holding gains depends on leadership's ability to develop and maintain a fact-driven measurement and audit system. Measurement is the bedrock of an organization. Measurements bring facts and articulate focus to what is important. Measurement is the "pulse" of what is going on. It is the essence of "the scoreboard."

## *You become what you measure!*

Measuring is one of the, if not the most, strategic things an organization does. Without measurement, how can performance be defined or people understand what is expected of them? Without measurement, organizations are running in the dark and operating by gut feel. Consistency and continuity are no better than the alignment of the next "educated guess" with the one immediately preceding it.

**MEASUREMENT**

What an Organization Measures

Determines ⬇

What Problems an Organization Sees

Determines ⬇

What Solutions It Chooses to Work On

Determines ⬇

What an Organization Does

Determines ⬇

**What an Organization IS !**

Ultimately, how an organization chooses to measure itself defines **what** that organization **is**. An organization's metrics are the sources of its rewards. People move to where the rewards are and stay away from where the rewards aren't. What gets measured gets worked on. Measurements signal variance from plan or aim. They are the basis for assessing progress and detecting problems. If satisfactory progress is being made, stay the course. If not, attack the "problem." Measurements elevate the problems organizations see. The problems it detects establish the boundaries for inclusion of possible solutions to implement. When the solution is selected and acted on, those activities define the behaviors and activities that are valued and rewarded. An organization's behavior and activity is its culture. Its culture is what it is.

An organization's leadership is accountable and has the authority for establishing the matrix of metrics that will define it. Organizations measure many things. However, the select few metrics its leadership pays attention to with their time and effort are the ones that drive the organization and define it. The higher the frequency of leadership attention to a measure, the more attention, focus, and energy organizations apply to the aspect being measured. Measurements are the flags for organizational improvement. The more attention leadership pays to any particular measure, the more vigorous the flag waving is perceived, and, in turn, the more organizational energy that is applied.

## *THREE is a Lonely Number*

At the core of checking is measurement and metrics. Lest you be swept away in the metric mania monsoons, keep in mind that for a metric to be useful, it must have three requisite attributes. First, it has to be *quantifiable*. Next, it must have a *known standard*. And last, it must be provided in a defined *context*. A metric is the quantification of facts organizations can accumulate about what can be seen. But a metric without a STANDARD has no meaning; and a metric and a standard without a CONTEXT has no significance.

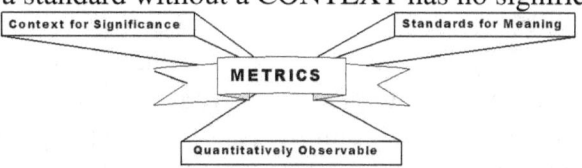

The number three is the quantification of discrete, observable things. Everyone knows that number 3 is larger than 2, and smaller than 4. Three is miniscule when compared to a hundred, and infinitesimal when compared to a million. But beyond that, it has no meaning or significance. If a standard is assigned to the number 3, such as feet, it takes on meaning. A foot is a measure of distance. It is equal to 1/3 of a yard or 12 inches, and is about 30½ centimeters. Three feet has meaning. It can be easily visualized, communicated, and understood. But, without a context, it has no significance. If the context of a running broad jump is applied to 3 ft., the significance of it (for an adult or teenager) is really no big deal. Grown people trip and fall that far. But, if the context is changed to that of a vertical leap, the significance of achieving a 3ft. vertical leap is a pretty big deal. A 3ft. standing vertical jump is in the league of world-class athletic performance.

Imagine standing up in front of an organization and declaring you are disappointed with last month's result of "three." Unfortunately, there is plenty of that going on: leadership advancing new metrics in the absence of clearly understood standards and meaningful context.

Without a standard that the organization can use to visualize the meaning or a context to judge the significance, what is it that you are saying? A leader advancing fuzzy metrics makes more of a statement about themselves than about the organization. New and improved metrics come on the scene, and they are quickly adopted by leadership as miracle cures, and they may well be. But deploying a new metric without a thorough organizational understanding of the standard, or without providing a connection to the context of the organization's aspirations has little or no meaning and even less significance.

## **The Paper Caper**

Back at Wiggly Lawn Ornaments Inc., Sam, the senior-purchasing guru and the Supplier Improvement Process Team were in high gear. After the initial bumpy team takeoff and getting Sam's behavior straightened out, things were going smoothly. The suppliers that the team had begun working with were a real case of the Good, the Bad, and the Ugly. Sam had read a lot about supplier convergence in Procurement periodicals. And once the team had broadened Sam's personal icon of supplier excellence beyond price alone, convergence for Sam was a pretty easy task. The Good won; the Bad got another chance; the Ugly were left behind. Sam had been able to visit a number of suppliers with the team during audits and discussions around increasing value and eliminating waste. Sam always had an eye out for "intelligence" on these visits. Sam was amazed at what some companies had on their walls. On one occasion, Sam came across a chart on the main office corridor that plotted the use of paper in that office section. Sam asked one of the office staff what that was all about. The response was, "That's how we measure our improvement. Before we started that we didn't know where we were or how we were doing. Now we're right on top of it. There's a funny story behind that graph. Remind me and I'll tell you after the meeting." Sam nodded in knowing agreement and turned back to look at the graph. The graph was dramatic. It looked like paper consumption had been cut in half in six months. Sam filed that statistic away and went off to the meeting.

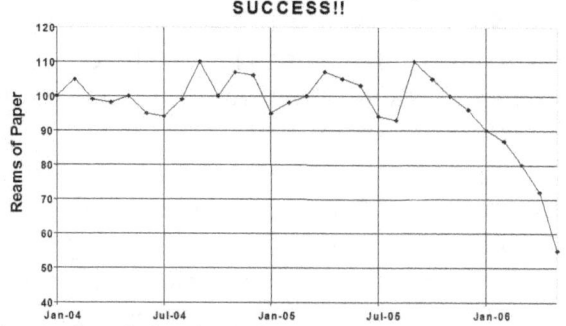

During a break in the meeting, Sam began wondering again about the graph. This was an impressive company. The energy level, enthusiasm, and morale were really high. Their products and services were outstanding when compared to the bulk of the suppliers the team had visited. "This paper consumption metric to measure office productivity must really have some merit," Sam thought. "Here is a company driving office productivity by driving down paper consumption. If office staff productivity could be measured by paper consumption, and less meant more, then maybe the end ought to be the means," Sam concluded. Sam had been itching to hit a "personal" home run for some time. This team thing was great, but nothing quite lived up to the feeling of launching one over the fence all by oneself. This metric seemed to be the pitch Sam had been looking for.

When the meeting broke up, Cathy, the person who had initially explained the chart to Sam in the hall, approached, saying, "Let me tell you about that Chart." Sam replied, "I'm impressed with the thinking behind that chart. Office productivity linked to paper consumption isn't something I've seen before." Cathy laughed. "That chart isn't really a direct measure of office productivity. But, that's the same mistake our VP made when he was on a site visit during a benchmarking study." Cathy continued, "The VP saw the same kind of chart, and when he got back from the site visit, he began a personal crusade to adopt it as a measure of office productivity. He even went as far as canceling reorders for paper as our stocks ran out to force people to communicate more productively." Cathy laughed again. "By the time the paper ran out, he had almost brought our company to its knees. We were a company whose work processes depended on paper. The company he had visited, unknown at the time to him, had recently transitioned to electronic communications. They were really measuring the rate of conversion from paper-based systems to electronic systems." Sam gulped. "Well, what are you using it for?" Cathy replied, "We recently installed an Intranet System company wide. The Intranet System is only part of a plan that is really going to impact our productivity. The reason why we're measuring paper consumption is because it's the best *indicator* of people getting up to speed with their computer skills and making progress moving away from paper to electronic communication."

Sam thanked Cathy profusely, and felt lucky that Cathy had stopped him to explain. Sam had already begun sketching out a plan in his head to cut back on paper purchasing to drive productivity before Cathy had stopped to explain the graph further. Sam thought, "I would have launched myself over the fence. Some homerun that would have been." Sam had learned that paper consumption, in this case, was a great metric. But, as Sam reflected, running off without a clear understanding of the standard or context around this measure would have been a disaster.

### Measure every which way.

Great measuring frameworks cascade metrics from top to bottom, and build up from bottom to top. The concept can easily be understood in the framework of financial measurement. An accountant can build up all the metrics, starting at the shop floor, and work them up to the ultimate "bottom-line." From that work-up, people can begin to understand and see the significance a particular period of performance (by the unit they are working within) had on the highest financial metric of the organization. But, in the context of the "scoreboard," it is a rare organization that has cascaded metrics down to the shop floor or clearly understood how shop floor actions build up and have an impact on the other three organizational stakeholders (Employees, Society, and Customers) and their organizational level metrics.

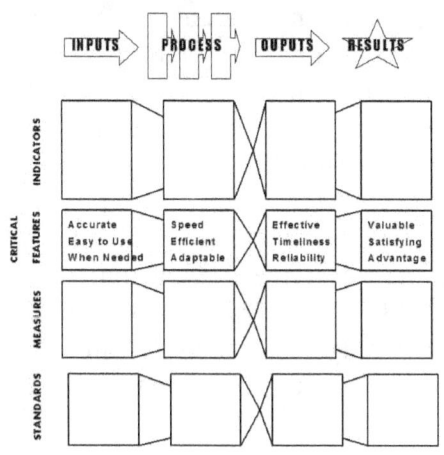

Great measuring frameworks measure performance not only vertically, but horizontally as well. In the model that follows, financial measurement is OUTPUT metrics oriented. While it is true that everything in a for-profit organization can be measured with money, the most common financial measures are output related. An output produces a RESULT. An Employee, Society, or Customer *Satisfaction* metric is RESULTS oriented. Outputs are what produce Results. Outputs come from a PROCESS that takes INPUTS and transforms them. Great organizational measuring frameworks measure all four elements – Inputs, Process, Outputs, and Results.

Great measuring and great metrics must connect and build horizontally. If you have a bad RESULT, the only thing that will change it is a modified or different OUTPUT. Outputs are the products of PROCESS and INPUTS. So, one or both of these must change for the Output to change and have an impact on the Result.

*Indicators* are what you can see and collect data around. *Critical Features* are the attributes of the indicators one should be concerned with. *Measures* are the quantifications of observable facts that have those critical features, and *Standards* are the basis for giving meaning and defining which way is up and which way is down.

Horizontal measuring enables organizational speed. An organization that only measures *Results* will be slower to discover a problem and its cause than an organization that measures not only *Results*, but the other three elements as well. If an organization receives a defective *input* or the *process* breaks down, there is no way in the world that the desired *product* can be produced, and no way that the *result* will be satisfactory. Organizations with limited measuring systems must wait for the "customer" of an output to report back that there is a problem. When organizations rely on that kind of measuring process, they not only lose valuable time and waste limited organizational resources, but worse, they *irritate customers*.

## *Indicators are easy to see if you look.*

Back at Harry's Haggle Corp., Harry et al. were on a roll. They had recognized their weakness and arrogance around customers and they were busily engaged in fixing it. They were also continuing to develop and build on their asset and technology strengths. But, Harry was worried again. "This Championing thing was really the way to go," Harry reflected to himself. "This organization is alive and focused." But, Harry stopped and wondered, "Are we really making progress with customer attitudes and our image, or are we just going through a lot of the motions?" Harry could see the bottom-line was improving, but "Was that only because Harry's Haggle Corp. was leveraging their low cost position to gain volume, and could they hold the gains they had made if a competitor started pushing back with price? How do we check what we've done and keep it in check?" he thought.

Harry went over to Lesli's office. Lesli had gone back to school and learned plenty about measuring an organization's work processes. She was now Haggle's' Measuring Champion and lead instructor. Harry had really been impressed with her presentations, and thought that if anyone could help him with his quandary, she could. So, Harry presented his worries and concerns, and asked what she thought. "Customer Satisfaction is an outcome of our overall business systems," she said. "That includes everything from order entry through delivery, as well as invoicing and billing, our practices around terms and accounts receivable, as well as after-sale service and support of their new product development efforts, and even down to how we answer the phone." Harry was beginning to regret having asked the question, but Lesli quickly canceled that emotion. Lesli continued, "Satisfaction is a feeling or perception. You really can't put a meter on it directly. Tell me, Mr. Huckster…" Harry interjected quickly, saying, "Please call me Harry." "O.K. Harry," Lesli continued, "when you like or are satisfied with something, what do you do or how could I tell? What would I look for you doing if I were a fly on the wall?"

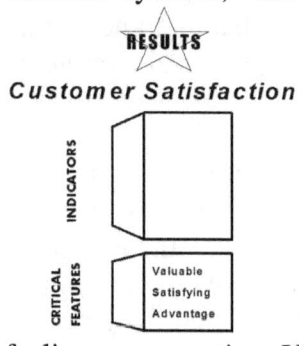

Harry thought about it a little and said, "Well, I would most likely be trying to get more of whatever it was I liked. And if I was really satisfied, I'd probably write a nice note to whoever it was that provided what it was that satisfied me. Maybe I'd even call them. For sure I'd be telling all my friends and acquaintances about it. If it was something that improved my golf game, I'd be slow to tell the three other people in my Saturday morning foursome about it until I'd paid for it in side bets."

Lesli interjected, "There really are a lot of things a person can observe about another that are indicators of whether that person is either satisfied or dissatisfied with something. We see it every day in our personal lives. What we don't typically do is accumulate observations and quantify what it is we are observing. That's what metrics and measuring is all about." Harry was beginning to feel a whole lot better.

### *Half baked is half baked*

As Harry was getting up to leave, Lesli said, "Please sit back down, Harry. You've asked the question, but I've only given you a partial answer." Harry almost said that he knew what to do now, but held his tongue. Lesli began again. "Once you get a handle on how to accumulate facts around the observable behaviors of customer satisfaction, you can't just stop there. You have to work backwards through our interactions with that customer, whether it is products or service, and then back through the processes by which we create them, whether factory or office, and finally to the inputs these processes use. You're looking for indicators all the way back to the beginning. Customer satisfaction today probably started out days or weeks, sometimes even months and years, before. Bottom line Harry," she concluded, "Unless we measure the complete bundle, we'll never really get a handle on checking Customer Satisfaction."

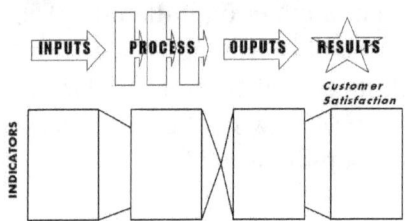

Harry pondered what Lesli had just told him. "So I guess an annual satisfaction survey like what Higgles Power Zone Inc. has started isn't going to cut it?" Lesli replied, "If that's all we do, we'll only be checking once a year. Is that feedback frequency going to give us the knowledge we need to accomplish what you've said we want to accomplish within the time frame you've laid out?" The answer was obvious, but the solution to the problem had just gotten a lot fuzzier. "You're right," Harry said. "What do you think we ought to do?" Harry had learned from championing that the fast track to involvement was asking for help. After a short discussion, Harry reached the conclusion that he and the SLT needed to charter a team to design a complete measuring system and metrics to monitor and observe the total package of customer satisfaction, inputs through results.

As Harry was leaving, he turned and asked, "I know you've been teaching this metrics and measuring thing to the rest of the organization, but would you mind if I assigned you as the team leader?" The expression on Lesli's face went from neutral into overdrive; he didn't need to even hear the answer. As Harry walked down the hall he reflected, "There is nothing like the commitment of those around you to ease a worried mind."

## *The Journey toward Wisdom*

An observable indicator of a *learning organization* is that it always keeps its gains in check, and it always continues to build on them.

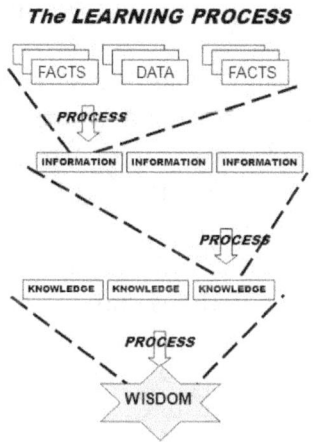

"Hold the gains" doesn't mean stop and dig in. It means pour on the fuel, learn, and leverage it. To hold a gain in check you first have to be able to detect that a gain has been made. That's ***data***. When you process data and render it down, you have ***information***. When you combine information with other information and look for patterns and insight, and you work to a higher level of understanding, that's ***knowledge***. When you combine streams of knowledge together with other streams of knowledge and boil it down further, you arrive at ***wisdom***. Organizational wisdom is the sense that leading organizations always seem to have that leads them to the right places at the right times with the right stuff. That sense isn't accidental or attributable to luck. It is there because of the continual systematic processing of their collective cumulative experiences.

There are many tools available to help organizations put a gain into check and hold it. They are the mechanics of standardization. But "mechanical" fixes, at some point, always seem to break down. In most cases, it is because the guardian of the fix is a person or persons, not the collective learning and wisdom of the organization. When the guardian leaves or moves on, the fix falls into a state of decay, and is soon abandoned. At this point, the process of learning re-zeros and begins all over again. As the saying goes, organizations that don't learn from their experiences are doomed to repeat them. And when the knowledge or wisdom around an aspect of operation is dispersed no further than a single person, it most surely will.

In a number of instances, the journey to organizational wisdom is cut short when the immediate problem is dealt with. The stopping of the processing of facts and data when the immediate problem goes away is a far too common norm of organizational behavior. Leadership that pulls an organization up-short and does not carry on the process of wringing out all the facts and data accumulated to kernels of knowledge disables the learning process. Organizations that do not have processes to combine and synthesize information streams to organizational knowledge, or processes to combine and extract wisdom from knowledge streams short-circuit organizational learning. An organization's leadership process is its core *learning* process as well. The *IMPLEMENTATION* Row of the leadership process model presented in Chapter VIII has auditing and order at its core.

Organizational learning and accumulated wisdom is the cement of organizational Ableness to check and retain the gains that have been accomplished. Outcomes that are variances from the expected are opportunities to learn, not something to be hidden, suppressed, or ignored.

## *Déjà vu*

After the *Reality Rally* at Higgles Power Zone Inc., the new Joe was really getting into leading. This rally had been a turning point for the better. Joe was now spending over 40% of his time out in the organization, walking around and mastering the Championing Tetrad. Joe was back at his old site one Friday morning, where "back in the day" he had been plant manager. He had been invited to sit in on the morning staff meeting so he could have a face-to-face dialogue about how things were progressing.

Just after the staff meeting began, the phone rang, followed shortly by a knock on the door. The plant manager's secretary explained that it was the same customer who, years before, when Joe had sat in the plant manager's seat, had called with a problem during a staff meeting. The customer needed to talk right away. It was happening again. Joe's whole management career flashed before his eyes as the new plant manager took the incoming call on the squawk box. The moment of truth was upon him. This call was going to be an audit of *HIM*. Had Joe's message been *clearly* communicated down to this level? Had people bought into it, and were they as *committed* as he now was? Was there still going to be *resistance* to move from the old norms of behavior he had led in the past? Was the incumbent plant staff going to distance themselves and pass the ball to him? "Am I ready to know the truth?" Joe ruminated to himself.

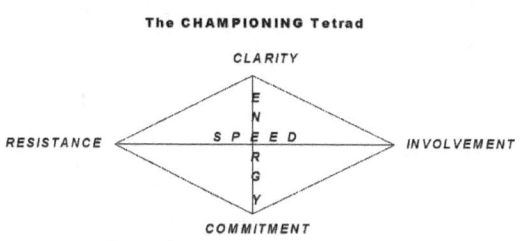

The truth came quickly and decisively, as truth has a habit of doing. Joe's message had gotten through and the staff was committed. There wasn't one sign of resistance, and the staff was totally involved with the customer's query to the point where Joe was an outsider to what was going on. As the call progressed, the customer's satisfaction with the response was readily apparent. As Joe watched, he observed a range of behaviors that continued to elicit favorable responses from the customer.

Joe had been dabbling with measurement. He was still struggling with the concept of *Indicators*, and was stuck with how to begin to objectively check his own leadership and that of every other Higgles Power Zone Inc. leader. Joe suddenly saw the answer playing out before his eyes. The leadership performance measurement survey formats Joe had previewed were focused on results, and were subjective in nature. A Results Survey was important, but how the results were produced was of equal or greater importance if he and the Higgles leadership were going to learn and get better. The Indicators of leadership are *behavior,* Joe suddenly realized. Behavior is something everyone can see and report on every day, not just at the end of the task, like results. As Joe thought about it further, the Behavioral Principles that he and his staff had embraced could be easily pocketed into either the Inputs block, Process block, or Outputs block of the mediating skill of leading. Joe's direction on leadership measurement was now clear.

When the phone call ended, Joe said to the staff, "You're already busy, and that phone call gave you more to do, not less. I've also found out what I needed to know, and it was presented in a clearer manner than any conversation could have accomplished. I'm proud of the way you all handled that call. I'll spend the rest of the morning wandering the floor and meet you all for lunch, which, by the way, is on me." With that, Joe left the meeting. He also left a new story that would guide the organization for years to come.

## *The tools of the trade*

The tools of measuring and checking are many. They range from simple Pareto Diagrams, Check Sheets, and Run Charts, to the more complex Control Charting and SPC. Whether simple or complex, they are essential to an organization's learning process. They demand quantifiable facts, and make organizations work to get them.

Organizations that strive to increase the factual basis of their decision making deploy these tools throughout, at all levels and around all aspects of their organization. Initially designed for manufacturing processes and processing the raw cold data from equipment and machinery, learning organizations have deployed them into all of their work process streams. SPC on Aim control charting can be equally effective in monitoring a sales process as it is a manufacturing factory process.

There are some fears of facts and statisticians that stem from the old adage of liars, where statisticians captured the highest place of "honor." Adages always have an element of truth, so it's wise not to blindly ignore them. But it's equally unwise to be hog-tied by these same adages. Some of the mischief of statistics is taking too little and making too much out of it. But the leverage of statistics is taking a little and getting a lot out of it. So where is the breakpoint? As a rule of thumb, statistical significance of a repetitive process begins somewhere in the realm of three dozen consecutive observations. Statistical relevance begins at about that point; less than that and you're dancing with irrelevance. While statistics aren't perfect, neither are gut instincts. Marrying the two can advance the cause of improvement more than either of these standing alone.

### *An Invention isn't an Innovation*

Back at Arlans' General, Billy Bob Neighbor, CEO, and the SLT were stuck on how to interpret changes they had introduced to the market in one of their core product lines. Everyone was looking at the same data, but they were split as to whether to declare victory or defeat. The entire Arlans team had spent a lot of energy trying to invent innovative ways to interact with the customers of this product line.

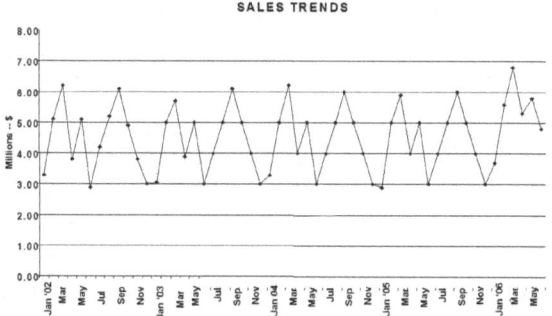

The people closest to the action were ready to declare what they had done a significant marketing innovation. The market had responded to their "inventions." On the one hand as the CFO put it, "This is just seasonal chatter. The only thing we invented was new ways to spend money."

The VP Marketing responded, "This is a major breakthrough. There is no doubt that we have innovated. The customers are responding, and our competitors will soon be forced to respond. If we don't go full speed ahead with this across all the product lines, we will lose the advantage against our competition!" After a bit more debate, Billy Bob intervened. "I don't know who's right or wrong, and neither does anyone else in this room for sure. The good news is that we are basing our discussion on factual data. The bad news is that, with the way the data is presented, we can't tell for sure. Let's let engineering take a look at it using SPC. This run chart is good, but we can do better." That seemed to satisfy everyone, and the SLT agreed they would get back together at the end of the day, after Engineering had a chance to analysis the data.

When they reconvened, Engineering presented the following control chart. "In a forensic kind of way we've processed the data using control chart technology as you asked. There are a couple of things we can say for sure. The last four years of sales have been fairly well 'in control,' around the yearly average. The seasonal buying swings are obvious, but that's part of the process for this product line. What's also clear is that something changed around the first of this year. There is a pronounced off Aim high alarm. Sales are up, and the increase is statistically significant. Something has happened. What we can't tell you is *how* or *why*."

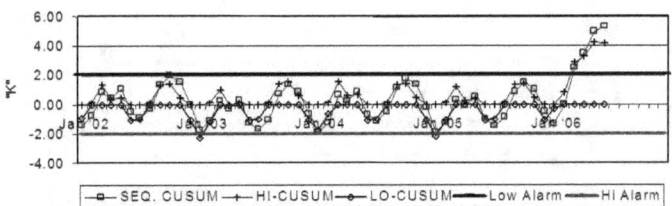

With that explanation, the engineering folks left, and the SLT was alone to renew the debate. Billy Bob cut in quickly. "This has helped, but it doesn't answer the question. We can say with certainty that sales are up, and this is not an aberration, so that part of the discussion is over. What we need to establish is whether there is a direct cause and effect relationship between our initiatives and response, measured by increased sales. If we are going to learn and get to a state of knowledge around this, we're going to have to combine this SPC analysis with other market information." The SLT quickly agreed. They also agreed that the SPC sales analysis was compelling enough to the have the PLT start planning the implementation of the suspected "innovation" across the board. "When we get the additional information we need collected, the PLT ought to be ready with a plan. If it's a go, we'll be right on top of it.

If it's a no-go, we'll at least have a generic plan for rapid, across-the-board implementation of future successful innovations." Billy Bob concluded, "I think we've also discovered an innovation on how to better process *data* to *information*. I also think we all ought to be on the lookout for unconventional ways to use conventional tools."

### ***Feeling the FORCE***

Keeping gains, a.k.a. learning, in check is critical to both the effectiveness and efficiency of organizations. An organization ought to only "pay for a learning" once. Continual payments for the same information or knowledge are a waste. Once learning is in check, it can be built upon and grown. "Learning" should not be compartmentalized or pocketed. Leverage is gained when learning from one aspect of an organization is extended to all other aspects. Learning developed by one part or function of an organization is, in many instances, of equal or greater value to other parts of an organization if and when they know about it.

# CHAPTER XI

## The HUMAN SIDE of IMPROVEMENT
## "... THROUGH PEOPLE ... "

IMPROVEMENT is about CHANGE. To understand and master improvement, you have to understand the dynamics of change. The word IMPROVEMENT denotes and connotes an image of BETTER. The word CHANGE does *not*, by definition, carry any implicative baggage of better or worse. If it does, in most instances it carries the watermark of worse. Regardless, people will always see and perceive improvement initiatives as *change*.

There are two kinds of CHANGE. The first is the ability to look different, yet remain the same. The change is only superficial in nature, and under the surface the substance remains unaltered. This is the kind of organizational change that becomes fodder for the comic strip broadsides. The practice of emulating the activities of a changed state without the substance is valid grounds for ridicule. It is not the type of change that results in competitive improvement.

Competitive improvement is about a different type of change. This second type attacks the "roots," the genetic makeup of an organization, and inalterably impacts it and is reflected in everything the organization is and does from that time on. It goes right to the values and behavioral principles of an organization and rewrites the codes. The competitive move from traditional vertical organizations to horizontal, from customer distancing to intimacy, from "do what I say" to empowerment, all require the rearticulating of values and the re-scripting of accepted behavior. Today's top-ranked competitive organizations are those that have learned this latter form of change. Both forms of change "cost" the same; one pays off in improved performance, and the other doesn't.

## *Show me the money!*

Haggle's was moving rapidly on many fronts since Harry had gotten refocused. Numerous things were being challenged and viewed from the new value set Harry was championing. One of them was Haggle's' ISO certification of their manufacturing operations. Haggle's had been certified for over a year now, but there were nagging questions and disappointment. As Harry and others saw it, Haggle's had gone through the expense of certification and continued maintenance, but nobody could spell out the payback. Cash out, no cash in. Harry said one day to staff, "Let's get the ISO team in here and ask them the questions about what's going on. We ought to be able to measure the impact in either increased revenue or share, or decreased cost. I just don't get it."

The ISO team came into a staff meeting a week later and Harry put the question to them. The team leader replied, "Bottom-line, all that ISO certification does is confirm we have a quality system, and that we follow it. For sure we touch all the bases we're supposed to, but it doesn't certify whether the system and our actions will have an impact. It's sort of like certifying that we have the roadmap, not so much what we do with it."

Harry was getting a little impatient and said, "What are you saying? If there is a message here, I'm not getting it." The ISO team leader was trying to be considerate, so he went back to the roadmap analogy. "What I'm saying is simple. If I give each of you an identical roadmap to get from here to Chicago, do you think everyone would get there at the same time, or at the same expense? Most likely not, because each of you would have different priorities and preferences, as well as varying driving and navigating skills. The same is true with ISO. We have the map, but our priorities, preferences, and skills aren't at the level that is going to produce what you're expecting."

Harry was really getting frustrated, but did manage to control himself. "Forget the roadmap stuff. Tell me in plain English what's wrong." The leader replied, "Our priorities around customer value and quality have not changed a twit from where they were 12 months ago, or 12 years ago. So, while the activities have changed, and the ISO certificate hangs on the wall, we're still the same company we always were!" Everything came into focus all at once for Harry. The roadmap, what Leslie the Measuring Champion had told him, and the Championing Tetrad, and how he hadn't really gone deep enough with what clarity, commitment, involvement, and resistance really were. Harry had been really feeling comfortable about the progress he thought had been made. This was a blow.

Harry said, "You're telling me we just aren't there yet?" The ISO leader replied, "Harry, we'll never be *there*. What you want and have been championing has no end point. It just has points along the way to bail out for those who don't want to continue. We are improving our frameworks, but until everyone embraces the values and principles that you do and their actions reflect that, we're not going to see the money."

Harry thanked the ISO team and, after they left, addressed the staff. "What they just told us is that if we quack like a duck, walk like a duck, and act like a duck, we're still a duck, regardless of how we dress ourselves up. A duck isn't going to win in our markets. We set the stage for improvement, but all we've been doing is *acting*. I've learned plenty here today. I learned that we can rearrange the furniture, change the setting, and change any other *physical* thing we want, but if we, the leadership, don't change our own values and behaviors and then get the rest of our associates to follow us, nothing much is going to happen."

## That's all well & good . . . but this is about me!

While improvement is all about change, change is about *CREATION*. Often forgotten or ignored by those engaged in the *improvement* process is (for those of us bound by the laws of science) that every act of creation is an act of *destruction*. For something to be created, the forms and essence of what once was must be dissolved. If you decide to cut down a tree, saw it into boards, and build a house, you can't undo it and get the tree back. It's that simple. However, the process of IMPROVEMENT is seldom thought about in the context of a process of *destruction*. But, that is exactly how all will perceive it at one point or another.

Sam at Wiggly Lawn Ornaments Inc. had experienced the destructive process of improvement. In very short order, Sam's "life" in purchasing had been turned upside down. One day, Sam was the standard of competence. Overnight, Sam was transformed into the definition of incompetence. Almost everything Sam knew and believed to be right about the "purchasing game" had been scuttled.

Improvement is a very destructive process. As Harry had just learned at Haggle's, improvement isn't skin deep. It goes to the bone. Competitive improvement is genetic. It gets down to the personal level of everyone who is involved; it attacks and challenges beliefs and long-held concepts of personal and organizational success. By its nature, it is disruptive and destructive, and demands response through individual action.

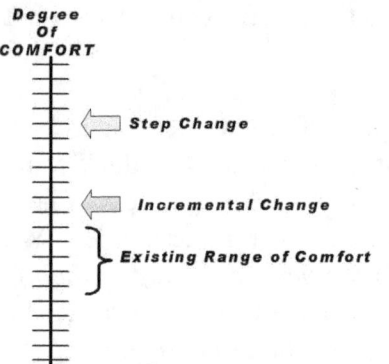

One of the most common attributes of improvement driven organizations is the continual activity of identifying and rooting out non-value-adding activity. Organizations that identify and strip out non-value-adding work many times get so immersed in the activity that they fail to recognize that they are stripping the identity and significance of those that were performing the work. Imagine the response of a person who discovers through an improvement team communication that their 20+year career has been spent at mastering non-value-adding work. Improvements may be easy to see on spreadsheets and process maps and charts, but more difficult to see and easier to ignore are emotions at the personal level. Changing the "process" is relatively simple when compared to dealing with the genetic issues of improvement, the human element of change. Organizations must provide a means and avenue for people to effectively move on.

Everyone is for improvement until the change impacts them personally. When it touches home, the destruction of "the way things were" has to be dealt with and reconciled. Those who are unable to reconcile it will resist it overtly or covertly. Covert resistance ranges from the behind-the-scenes forms of active resistance to that which is more difficult to uncover and deal with: subconscious passive resistance. The overly pragmatic and the outright procrastinators take a wait-and-see position. "We've been through these fads before!" For the doubting Thomas type, it is "show me." Resistance comes in many forms, from intellectual to emotional. Intellectual resistance can be facilitated with fact and logic. No such technical facilitation exists for emotional resistance except patience and perseverance.

The difference in difficulty between incremental change and step change is more about effectively dealing with the previously-mentioned people aspects of improvement than it is about the mechanics. Successful improvement demands high levels of personal conviction, displayed through commitment and perseverance. The greater the improvement envisioned, the greater the commitment and the greater the tenacity required. While step-change improvements come quickly when they occur, the front-end demands and work leading up to them are extensive in terms of people preparation.

Step change improvements are rare because of the need for a fundamental rock bottom commitment to truly let go of the "way things have been," to move out of personal comfort zones. It is difficult and it comes with risk. But not making a commitment to change is also a risk, sometimes the greater risk, depending on the vigor of present competition and, more strategically, future competition.

### *Is there a leader in the house?*

Improvement is something that can only be led. Attempts to manage or boss change fail to get at the genetics of an organization. There may be a modeled response to comply and stay out of harm's way, but without continued superior/subordinate interaction and intervention there is always a reversion to the way things had been. The improvement wanted is never held.

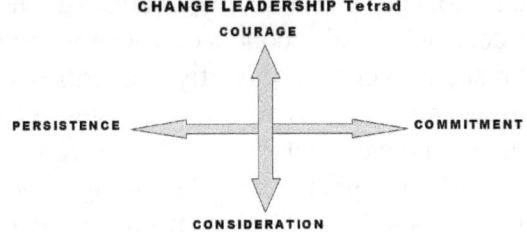

Genetic change requires leadership. The dynamics are interconnected and reciprocally support one another. They revolve around four demonstrated leadership behaviors -- commitment, persistence, consideration, and courage, as presented in this model. Consideration without courage is capitulation. Courage without consideration is domination. Persistence without commitment is vacillation. Commitment without persistence is resignation. Courage combined with commitment speaks to leadership integrity. Persistence linked with courage delivers leadership intent. Persistence in the context of consideration gives guidance to those that observe. Consideration in balance with commitment determines effectiveness.

Every single act of leadership in an improvement effort must embrace all four attributes. Leadership behavior embracing courage, commitment, and persistence in the absence of consideration incites rebellion. Conversely, consideration, persistence, and commitment without courage will result in stop/start, recycle, and organizational energy drain. Leadership demonstrating courage, commitment, and consideration, and not persistence fosters wait-and-see. Consideration, courage, and persistence without commitment are the source of activity traps, the endless do-loop syndrome. The personal leadership dynamic is always there to be dealt with. Failing to acknowledge or address all four aspects results in less than desirable outcomes.

## *Getting to critical mass*

Organizational *improvement* is accomplished *through people*. The Championing Tetrad is an external organizational view of improvement dynamics, while the Change Leadership Tetrad is a personal internal leadership perspective. The marriage of the two shares a common ground, ***commitment***.

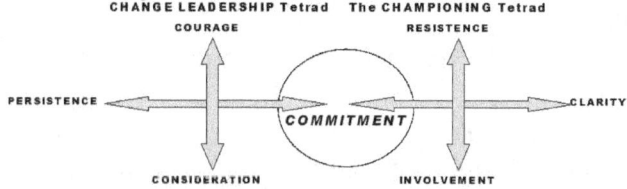

Improvement can't be accomplished without people, and more to the point, it can't be accomplished without the commitment of all the people within an organization. Organizational commitment without leadership commitment won't work, just as leadership commitment without organizational commitment doesn't work in improvement implementation. They feed on and build on each other. The higher the organizational commitment builds, the easier it is for leadership to demonstrate courage, persistence, and consideration. Conversely, the higher the level of leadership commitment demonstrated, reinforced with leadership's persistence, consideration, and courage, the easier it is for organizations to deal with their resistance, seek out and obtain necessary clarity, and become personally involved.

Any improvement has to achieve a critical mass at the onset for success to be possible. This critical mass can be measured, audited, and assessed through the *indicators* of leadership and organizational *commitment*. The greater the improvement attempted, the greater the critical mass required. The indicators of commitment are most easy to see, quantify, and measure in the formal and informal communication processes of an organization. If the communication level surrounding the improvement is insignificant compared to the mass of other organizational communication, what does it say about the owners of the formal communication processes, the organization's leadership commitment? While formal communications processes are the activating forces of improvement, the informal communication processes (the grapevine and rumor mill) are the responding forces. Organizations need to pay attention to both these processes and take guidance from the objective measurable feedback around commitment that is available for those who seek it.

## *Fear of Flying*

The single largest restraint at the onset of an improvement initiative is fear, specifically fear of failure. From a leadership standpoint, this means asking, "Will I be able to lead this change?" or "What if this doesn't produce the results we hope for?" The fear is real. Leadership has the authority and accountability. From the standpoint of those that would be led, the questions are "Will I be successful in my new role?" or "Will I fit in?" Those fears are equally real.

The root cause of these fears can be found in the *Success Triangle*. They are embedded in understanding and Ableness, "I know," and "I can." When the two are combined, they become **competency**. Organizations owe their people the means to develop and achieve competency not only in fulfilling their existing roles, but also in the new roles that continue to emerge in an improvement driven organization. People owe their organizations a dedication to continually expand their knowledge and skills in ways that contribute to the ongoing success of the organization.

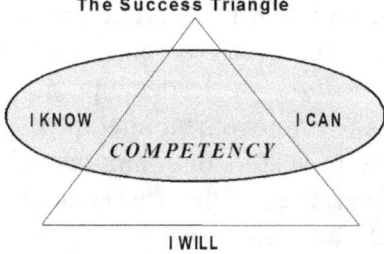

The decisive factor in organizational success today is rapidly moving away from traditional emblems of capital (equipment, technology, low cost labor, etc.) to the new capital of organizational know-how and skill. The traditional emblems are increasingly accessible to anyone, but this new form of capital is not. Dealing with the fears of improvement, and building the Ableness and competence of all people within an organization is a critical success factor. In many cases, the cost of eliminating a negative is only an offset. In this case, eliminating fear of change, a negative, through developing a competency for change is more than a quid pro quo offset. It dramatically increases the leverage for achievement. *The root cause of fear within an environment of improvement is perceived potential for personal incompetence.* The only way to stamp out fear is through developing and building competency.

### *Yeah . . . right!*

Cynicism is a systemic barrier to improvement that prevails to one degree or another in all organizations. If allowed to grow unchecked, it can kill. Cynicism's roots lie in the belief that that the conduct of another is motivated wholly by self-interest. It is a disbelief in the sincerity of others. Cynicism's symptoms range from degrees of organizational paralysis to organizational death. Wars are always supported by campaigns of propaganda that fuel the fires of cynicism. Cynicism is the antithesis of unity. Cynicism and unity compete for the same mental space. An organization's MENTAL SPACE can't be filled simultaneously with both cynicism and unity. One displaces the other. The only route to decreasing one is increasing the other. An organization can't work on stamping out cynicism, but it can work on building and increasing unity.

The path to unity traverses three distinct phases -- openness, then understanding, and finally caring. It's impossible to care or be motivated to do something about a situation one doesn't understand or comprehend. And without openness, it's impossible to develop understanding. Cynicism exists vertically and horizontally in organizations. It impedes vertical and horizontal trust. In unity there is trust; without trust there cannot be unity.

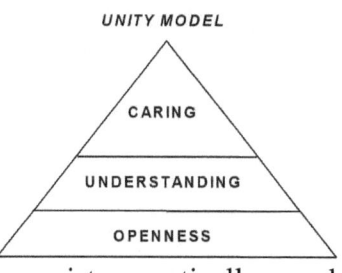

Cynicism is the fuel of mistrust and suspicion. Unity is the fuel of organizational speed. The foundation of Unity is Openness, whose bedrock is *disclosure*. Unity is difficult to achieve because of personal aversion to disclosure. Disclosure involves risk: the risk of non-acceptance, the risk of ridicule, the risk of being wrong. But, without disclosure, the journey to unity can't begin. People have learned the behavior of holding their "cards close to the vest." That behavior has to be unlearned. Nondisclosure is the turf of organizational politics. Organizational politics are the apex of non-value-adding work. One of the best indicators of organizational unity (or better put – lack of it) is the quantification and the measurement of political behavior. World-class organizations <u>are not</u> highly internally political; the "also-rans" are.

## *Mastery*

The people of an improvement-minded organization must cultivate and become masters of change. An organization that has been lulled to sleep by its historic position and competitive relationships finds it very difficult to respond to an upstart competitor whose cultural foundation is steeped in change. Entrepreneurial spirit thrives on change. New competitive entries based on this don't follow the same rules as organizations that are well in place. They succeed by changing the rules of the game, by seeing the market in a whole different way. They succeed by tilting the Fair Value Line in the Value/Price dynamic of the constituents they serve. They disrupt the marketplace status quo with innovation. In many instances, their entry causes a shakeout, and those who can't respond with speed fall by the wayside.

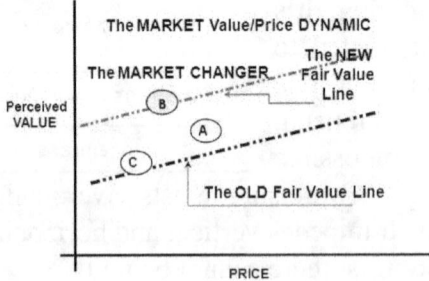

The regeneration of Arlans' General through the entrepreneurial spirit that Billy Bob Neighbor brought illustrates that an entrepreneurial company doesn't have to be a newcomer to a market or competitive playing field. To be an entrepreneur is to embrace a mindset and behavior that accepts risk, accountability, and responsibility. Arlans' General came in and disrupted the Value/Price relationship that had existed. Arlans' General took a risk by going after what could be. It was quickly accepted by customers as what should be. They did not accomplish this through new equipment or technology. They did it through developing and utilizing the skills and behavior of the people of Arlans' General. Specifically, they developed people with the ability to self-manage authority, accountability, and responsibility in a way that mitigates risk.

### ***What you are isn't what you were or will be***

There is a life cycle of organizational forms. The inability of an organization to make change, improve, and regenerate itself into newer, more effective and efficient competitive forms is a frequent cause of organizational death. While the life cycle of products and services has been cut from decades to years and months in recent times, the life cycles of organizational forms having similar time frames is on the horizon. An organizational competency in regenerating itself is a competitive advantage. It may be the only competitive advantage that is sustainable. It is so difficult to replicate. This competency resides within the organization's human resources, its people, from top to bottom.

The notion of flexible manufacturing, the ability of a function to bend and adapt, yet retain its core strength in the face of ever-changing demands, has been heralded for many years. At the heart of it is the design of physical assets.

The era of flexible organizations, the ability of an organization to reform and adapt itself to competitive environmental and customer evolution and revolution, is already here. At the heart of this ability is the skill and capability of leadership and human resources to successfully execute change.

The vertical organization is dead or dying in all but the least-advanced competitive cultures. It does not have the compensating speed or efficiencies to compete with an amorphous horizontal organization that rapidly adapts, yet is able to retain its strengths for leverage and advantage. Whom do I report to and where do I place allegiance drives vertical organizations that, in turn, defines the compartments and performance measurement.

Functional or vertical chains of command do not compartmentalize horizontal organizations with walls. The role of functions in horizontal organizations is to define and provide continued skill growth and increased competency in their areas of expertise. Integrated business and work processes that enable the whole to stay in constant contact with customers, competition, and environments, regardless of function, are what drive horizontal organizations. These organizations can immediately see and act in response to external needs. They regenerate themselves in real time as the problems and situations they face develop. Developing this competency is a competitive power not easily matched.

# FINALE

Balladeers have forever crooned the loss of "that loving feeling." In the same way, organizational leaders find themselves bemoaning the loss of "that improvement feeling." Balladeers use vibrant **VERBS** to portray their actions in the search and recovery of the "feeling" lost. If it works for them, it ought to work for us.

"THE VERBS OF CHANGE" in Chapters V - X was a portrayal of the actions and **BEHAVIORS** of people in an **IMPROVEMENT PROCESS**. They are the words one typically should be using to answer the question, "What did you do today?" If you've lost that "improvement feeling," look back and see which one of these **VERBS** you've lost. If you're just starting, these are the kinds of behaviors you can expect to cycle through, over and over. When you are talking about the "rate of improvement," don't forget that most will understand you as saying the "rate of change"; all will hear (at one time or another), the "rate of destruction."

In a competitive environment, standing still is tantamount to losing ground or moving backward. Going "on hold" isn't an option; in almost every instance it's an irresponsible and inconsiderate choice. Even so, it doesn't make choosing to move ahead or improve faster than the competition a no-brainer to implement.

So pick from the fantastic tools, techniques, methods, and means available for making improvement. Use this book to *self-examine* your own personal behavior and style, and as a help to you to *remember* how you should feel and behave as you are using the many means of improvement. No matter what improvement model you follow, keep the visceral *VERBS of CHANGE* in mind, because they are the ones people respond to in a change/improvement process.

Ring the *bells* loudly, make your *voice* heard, and create great *stories*.

Always remember that if you aren't paying attention to your actions and the stories those actions create everyone else is.

**About the Author**
Joe Schmid is the Managing Principal of Oak Leaf Consulting, LLC (www.oakleafconsulting.com). He has over 40 years of business experience with a background in change leadership and developing high performance organizations. Joe has held positions as Plant Manager, VP of Manufacturing and Engineering, VP/GM; and a corporate board member. He earned his Bachelor's Degree in Mechanical Engineering from the University of Detroit. Joe is the author of *If You Are What You Eat, Your Company Is What It Thinks*.

www.ingramcontent.com/pod-product-compliance
Lightning Source LLC
Chambersburg PA
CBHW051650170526
45167CB00001B/413